KNOWING & DOING

IN HEIDEGGER'S

BEING & TIME

◎

"This is an excellent translation of an original and provocative critique of the 'theo-reticism' of pure knowledge. Prauss sees in Heidegger's 'Being and Time' the only promising attempt since Kant's first efforts to develop a compelling account of the interdependence of knowing and doing. Even those who do not share Prauss's Kantian dualism and his misgivings about Heidegger's account will find his painstaking conceptual and systematic analysis of the correlation between knowing and doing intriguing. It is a boon for epistemologists, Kant scholars, and Conti-nental philosophers alike. But most of all, it is an unexpected and challenging con-tribution to the ongoing debate of the central issue of classical American philosophy that has been revived by the neo-pragmatists, namely, the integration of knowing and doing."

Hans Seigfried, Department of Philosophy, Loyola University of Chicago

"Those who have learned to approach Heidegger through lenses provided by Gadamer, Derrida, and their many followers may well be disappointed by this brief, admirably clear and sober text, which suggests that the most promising way to Hei-degger leads through Kant. But Prauss's 'practicism' deserves careful consideration not just as a critical, yet sympathetic response to Heidegger, but as a challenging contribution towards a transcendental theory of action."

Karsten Harries, Department of Philosophy, Yale University

"Prauss raises questions that have long been overlooked by Heidegger's followers, and which need to be asked. The English version is both faithful and smooth. The translators have done a real service to Continental philosophy in the English-speaking world."

David Carr, Department of Philosophy, Emory University

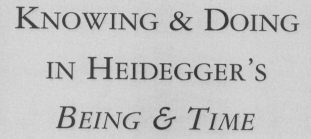

KNOWING & DOING IN HEIDEGGER'S *BEING & TIME*

GEROLD PRAUSS

Translated by
Gary Steiner and Jeffrey S. Turner

Humanity Books

an imprint of Prometheus Books
59 John Glenn Drive, Amherst, New York 14228-2197

Originally published in German as *Erkennen und Handeln in Heideggers "Sein und Zeit"*
© Verlag Karl Alber Freiburg München 1977

The essay "Heidegger and Practical Philosophy" by Gerold Prauss was previously published as "Heidegger und die Praktische Philosophie" aus *Heidegger und Die Praktische Philosophie.* Herausgegeben von Annemarie Gethmann-Siefert und Otto Pöggeler, Seiten 177–90 © Suhrkamp Verlag Frankfurt 1988.

Published 1999 by Humanity Books, an imprint of Prometheus Books

03 02 01 00 99   5 4 3 2 1

Library of Congress Cataloging-in-Publication Data

Prauss, Gerold.
    [Erkennen und Handeln in Heideggers "Sein und Zeit." English]
    Knowing and doing in Heidegger's "Being and time" / Gerold Prauss; translated by Gary Steiner and Jeffrey S. Turner.
        p.   cm.
    Includes bibliographical references and index.
    ISBN 1-57392–670–1 (cloth)
    1. Heidegger, Martin, 1889–1976. Sein und Zeit. 2. Ontology. 3. Space and time. 4. Act (Philosophy) 5. Knowledge, Theory of. I. Title.
B3279.H48S466713   1999
111—dc2l   97–30140
                                                                          CIP

Printed in the United States of America on acid-free paper

Contents

circumspection—a "sight" that is nonetheless still to be understood as a kind of concern. Thus knowing and doing threaten "to collapse into one another under the rubric of 'concern' " (p. 3 below). Furthermore, (2) in ¶ 69 (b) of *Being and Time* Heidegger himself ends up *criticizing* the "deficiency" account of the origin of theoretical knowing of the present-at-hand from practical dealings with the ready-to-hand—although Heidegger himself is not explicit about the fact that he is criticizing the very view he has already put forward in *Being and Time*.

Now, if knowing and doing threaten to collapse into one another when understood simply as "concern," then not only must doing presuppose a kind of knowing (viz., circumspective "sight") but knowing must presuppose a kind of doing. And, as Prauss points out in his second chapter, Heidegger does indeed claim in ¶69 (b) of *Being and Time* that natural science has its own practice; but surprisingly, Heidegger is not talking about *technology* there but instead only about things like the preparations necessary for observing through a microscope. *Being and Time* itself, unlike the later Heidegger, has no hint of the insight that the real essence of modern natural science is technology, because it conceives of natural science as θεωρία in Aristotle's sense (see p. 9). This means that after *Being and Time* Heidegger really makes a "shift" (*Wende*) that is even more fundamental than his well-known "turning" (*Kehre*): a shift in his understanding of the relations between knowing and doing or theory and practice, since he now comes to understand theory not as purely receptive θεωρία but instead as itself having practical "import" (*Einschlag*)—namely, technology.

Prauss's third chapter, "The Primacy of Knowing over Doing," tries to show three things: that Heidegger's attempt to establish a primacy of practice over theory fails; that what Heidegger's failure here really shows is a primacy of theory over practice; and that the two interpretations of Heidegger's *Being and Time* mentioned above (viz., what one might call Tugendhat's "pragmatic" interpretation and Bröcker's "dissolution" interpretation) do not really contradict one another but instead "stand in an inner connection" (p. 22). Heidegger's attempt to establish a primacy of practice over theory must fail because circumspection must be perception, and such perception must perceive something determinate; because Heidegger's notion of "pre-predicative understanding" is both itself inconsistent and also inconsistent with other claims in *Being and Time* (see pp. 15–17), this perception must then be interpreted as a knowledge of the present-at-hand. This opens up the space for one to see that Heidegger's whole notion of "concern" is problematic, since concern for Heidegger is really understood only as doing or practice. Thus it is no wonder that Heidegger has such difficulty trying to articulate the "change-over" from practice to theory, from dealings with the ready-to-hand to knowledge of the present-at-hand.

Thus Heidegger fails to show two things in *Being and Time*: "a pure circumspection regarding the ready-to-hand which is still not knowledge of the present-at-hand, and a pure knowledge of the present-at-hand which would no longer be circumspection regarding the ready-to-hand" (p. 25). In "The Theory of 'Disturbed' Concern," the fourth chapter of *Knowing and Doing*, Prauss begins to try to show how his revision of Heidegger's position has "substantive and systematic" import for the problem of theory and practice. A close look at the things that Heidegger designates as "deficient modes" of concern in *Being and Time* shows that he fails to see there that "disturbed" concern is really *failed or unsuccessful* concern. This leads Prauss to the claim that knowing and doing cannot be dissolved into one another, because "success" or "failure" properly applies only to action, while "truth" or "falsity" applies properly only to knowing. We could, metaphorically, speak of "successful" or "unsuccessful" knowing—this brings out something implicit in the nature of knowing, viz., the practical import of theory—but we could not speak of "true" or "false" doing without ignoring "a fundamental difference between knowing and doing or theory and practice" (p. 30).

As oriented toward success, then, knowing and doing are to be understood as kinds of *intentionality*, and Prauss proceeds to offer a revision of the understanding of knowing in terms of *noesis* (the act of knowing) and *noema* (the content of knowing). Only the noesis can be something intentional, and the noesis always intends to succeed: it makes no sense, Prauss claims, to intend falsity or failure. Thus, as opposed to Marxist "ideology" or Freudian "repression," there is a "strict" or "fundamental" dichotomy between error and lie: error is still an instance of knowing, while a lie is something *done*. Prauss concludes this chapter by clarifying the "practical import" of theory or knowing, which he identifies as knowing's intention to succeed. And so when doing fails, this is intelligible only because the relevant knowledge has failed; when it succeeds, that is intelligible only in terms of the success of its guiding (circumspective) knowledge. Thus knowledge or theory is to be understood as the *means* to successful activity or practice.

But what is this character of knowing as a "means" to activity? In the fifth chapter, Prauss analyzes the nature of such "means" and hence thinks through some of Heidegger's central claims about "equipment" in *Being and Time*. His central claim is that, contra Heidegger, it is not *the beings* in our environment *themselves* that are means, but the grasping or, more generally, *dealing with them* that is the means to activity. The transposition of this character from our activity to the beings themselves is a kind of "fallenness," in something like Heidegger's sense: Heidegger himself falls into interpreting beings in terms really appropriate only to Dasein. Thus his conception of ready-to-hand equipment in our environment "borders closely on an occult conception of the environment" (p. 37).

Prauss nonetheless qualifies this claim by attempting to show what he calls the "real primacy of doing over knowing," namely, that knowing is not simply directed toward the actual itself, as Aristotelian θεωρία might be, but "knowing is instead *nothing but* the way in which doing directs itself toward what is already actual" (p. 41, our emphasis). Only this will allow us to understand why the metaphor of an "act" of knowledge is justified, while the converse metaphor of "true" or "false" doing is unjustified. Prauss therefore aims toward "a complete 'transcendental' theory of subjectivity" (p. 43), and he ends this chapter by distinguishing, through an extension of the noesis/noema distinction to one between *poiesis* and *poiema*, the senses in which doing has a primacy over knowing and knowing has a primacy over doing.

The final two chapters of *Knowing and Doing* attempt to put this substantive and systematic revision of Heidegger's thought into the context of issues Heidegger raises after *Being and Time*, and also attempts to situate this revision with respect to important philosophical discussions in Germany in the last third of this century, particularly those between "critical theorists" and "critical rationalists." More specifically, Prauss claims that his view amounts to "a practicism of knowing and truth" (p. 47), according to which "[a]s actual things in the environment, beings are as a matter of fact always perceived by Dasein from the start with an eye toward what can be done with them" (p. 47). Heidegger had turned away from such a practicism, toward the "utopian backwardness" of a pure theoreticism. But finally Heidegger's own insights into science and technology would lead him, Prauss claims, back in the direction of practicism, and away from conceptions of a purely receptive perceiving and truth as "unconcealedness"—conceptions of antiquity which Kant showed to be outmoded. To understand humanity requires, then, the modern notion of subjectivity.

This does not mean, though, that we should let subjectivity's relentless pursuit of success simply have sway over us. Nor should we recoil from practicism and retreat into Heidegger's utopian theoreticism. Instead we should face up to practicism and "confront subjectivity . . . with the problem of morality" (p. 57). This would amount to a recognition that subjectivity "from the start . . . is always essentially something bifurcated" (*jeweils von vornherein und wesentlich in sich gebrochen*) (p. 60), rather than something "straightforwardly natural" (*einer ungebrochenen Naturwüchsigkeit*), as the materialists one-sidedly believe. Subjectivity is bifurcated from the start, as Kant had maintained, because no matter how arbitrary it may wish to be in its doing, in its knowing it must still aim for objectivity. (The most radical revolutionaries as well as the most ardent supporters of the National Rifle Association want their weapons built according to physical principles about "the way things are," one might say.) "Critical theorists," though on the right track in stressing the primacy of doing over knowing, fail to see that "subjectivity" (in the sense of "being merely subjective," i.e., arbitrary) in the noetic-poietic sense does not entail such "subjectivity" with respect to the noema and poiema.

Knowing and Doing ends with the suggestion that the view Prauss has developed might offer the possibility of securing the moral law "against the suspicion of illusion or even of ideology"—a possibility whose practical import would be so important that Prauss need do no more than hint at it there. In "Heidegger and Practical Philosophy," published in 1988, Prauss both brings together the central threads of his argument in *Knowing and Doing* and deepens its discussion of the theory of subjectivity. With regard to the former task, then, this essay serves as a nice conclusive summary to that work, as Prauss deepens his discussion of the regressive character of Heidegger's later thought—its appeal to ancient-medieval concepts rather than modern ones (see pp. 68–70), and its complete retreat from the theory of action—and once again points in the direction of "a thoroughgoing practicity the extent of which had never before been known" (p. 68), either by the German Idealists or by their successor Heidegger.

With regard to the latter task, the deepening of the discussion of the theory of subjectivity, and from there into the foundations of ethics, Prauss focuses in particular on developing a critique of some of Heidegger's comments on technology. Prauss notes that Heidegger fails to see that the overgrowth of technology is not the same as the "hypertrophy of a beehive or an ant hill," because he fails to see "that in technology subjectivity is practical, that is, subjectivity proceeds from its autonomy and seeks success intentionally" (pp. 71f.). And so too in ethics: by missing the importance of the subjectivity of the subject, Heidegger, with his "step back" into θεωρία, fails to see that subjectivity *as moral autonomy* "is concerned with restraining one's intentionality and with mastering one's lust for success" (p. 72).

CRITICAL RESPONSES TO PRAUSS'S ARGUMENT IN *KNOWING AND DOING IN HEIDEGGER'S "BEING AND TIME"*

Given the stress that Prauss places on Heidegger's failure to engage in a self-critique that could have led to a viable theory of action, it should not be surprising that Prauss himself lodged a criticism of the argument of his own text not long after it appeared. In his text on Kant's theory of freedom, Prauss says that he erred in *Knowing and Doing* when he conceived of knowing as an intention directed at something already actual rather than as an intention directed at something not yet actual.[21] Knowing, precisely like doing, involves an intention to change something, and this must be recognized in order to see the *full* extent to which knowing "has the character of practicity."[22]

Apart from this self-critique, several more fundamental criticisms have been made of Prauss's argument in *Knowing and Doing*. All of these criticisms touch in one way or another on Prauss's attempt to construe circumspection as a viewing of the present-at-hand. And this should not be surprising, given that such an interpretation appears to be deeply at odds with much of what Heidegger says about circumspection in *Being and Time*. In a book review published shortly after the release of Prauss's text, Peter Rohs raises a question about Prauss's notion of practicism that touches upon this theme in an indirect way.[23] Prauss defines the noema in two ways, namely, as something into which the noesis forms itself, and as the manner in which the noesis either forms itself into something true (and hence is successful) or forms itself into something false (and hence is unsuccessful).[24] Rohs takes this to mean that the noema is both a way in which spontaneity acts (which is to be understood as the intention to succeed) and is itself the result of an act of spontaneity. The latter sense of spontaneity

> must be foundational for knowing, since of course all intersubjectivity is rooted in it. And I wonder whether this [latter sense of spontaneity] too can be understood adequately as a "directedness toward success." Surely (as Prauss emphasizes) there can be no success in doing without success in knowing, and there can be no success in knowing without the noema. But that does *not* mean that the act of forming itself [on the part of the noesis] is an activity that is directed towards success (for in this connection, success would consist in the formation of the noema and failure would consist in its not taking place). It does not seem to me that this kind of noema can be the content of an intention to succeed. And it is also unclear what contribution would be made to our understanding of this particular kind of spontaneity, if we were to subsume it under that rubric. For this would not explain how a noema can come into being through self-formation on the part of the noesis. It seems to me that the possibility of this achievement cannot be explained on the basis of an intention to succeed, but on the contrary that the intending of success would be possible only on the basis of such an achievement.[25]

For Rohs, this means that "there must be a form of spontaneity that cannot be conceived as an 'act' and hence is unintelligible [when understood] as the 'intention of a subject to succeed'—i.e. [when understood] as self-formation into the noema."[26]

Rohs does not explain exactly how we *should* understand that manner of spontaneity which is directed first of all at truth rather than at success in changing the world, but his suggestion seems to be that knowing is to be understood in terms of something other than intentionality. This suggestion implicitly raises the question whether knowing would be better understood in terms of Aristotelian θεωρία, which Prauss rejects for being all too detached from the practical contexts in which knowing occurs first of all and most of the time. Prauss sees the prospect of understanding circumspection as a sighting of the present-at-hand; but in doing so, he wants to avoid the implication that circumspection is anything like θεωρία. Notwithstanding Prauss's powerful insight into human practicity, Rohs's criticism implicitly raises the difficult question whether circumspection can be understood as a sighting of the present-at-hand without at the same time being understood in terms of θεωρία rather than in terms of an intentional noesis that is dependent upon a poiesis.

Reinhold Aschenberg touches more directly upon this question in his criticism of Prauss's argument for the practicism of *Being and Time*:

> The practicistic thesis that a subject intends the results of his intellective efforts solely as a means to obtain success in his actions (34, 47) is in no way equivalent to the claim, which is as pertinent as it is trivial, that knowing possesses a hint of praxis and that also in the act of knowing the intention of the subject is directed toward a result (the truth) (32). In the case of knowing, the intended result is a purely *theoretical* one; the intention to obtain knowledge possesses a "hint of praxis" only in the metaphorical and harmless sense that here, too, a "result" (unmetaphorically: the truth) is intended. The question of whether in reality all knowing is only a means for praxis or whether there does not rather exist something like self-sufficient knowing in the Aristotelian sense of *theoria* remains accordingly open.[27]

Aschenberg's criticism of Prauss's practicistic interpretation of *Being and Time* explicitly raises the question whether Prauss is justified in arguing that all knowing ultimately takes place for the sake of doing; and Aschenberg points out that "even when one grants the interdependence of knowing and doing what follows from this is that action can be directed towards a real thing only through knowing something about it, and not that therefore all knowing is solely a means of action and directed toward the real only in the interest of success in some act upon it."[28]

An additional question that Aschenberg might have raised in this connection is whether Prauss is justified in arguing that Heidegger is forced, if only against his own intention, to the conclusion that circumspection is fundamentally a sighting of the present-at-hand. For Heidegger does a great deal of work in *Being and Time*, and in his lecture course from the winter semester of 1925–26, to attempt to demonstrate a phenomenological distinction between the hermeneutic and the apophantic "as"; and much of his purpose in doing so is to make a case for the idea that circumspective seeing grasps not objective features of things but rather the involvements that those things have in a pre-predicatively meaningful totality.[29] Is it not worth questioning whether there is, as Heidegger attempted to demonstrate, more than one sense of seeing "as" at work in cases in which we "grasp" a hammer? One such sense would be the apophantic sense of grasping a hammer cognitively, the other sense would be the hermeneutic sense of grasping a hammer practically, purely in terms of its involvement in a totality of reference, for example, with the intention of driving in a nail with it. Do we really "see" the hammer in the same way in the two instances? In effect, Prauss rejects the possibility that there could be an "as" that is hermeneutic or pre-predicative.

Aschenberg raises two additional criticisms, both of which are of fundamental consequence for Prauss's entire argument. First, Aschenberg points out that Prauss's practicism leaves him with

> the problem faced by every defensible practicism . . . namely, that the theory by which to establish that practicism must in turn be valid. This theory is itself obviously not praxis and the question of its validity—and along with this the question of the correctness of the assertion of the primacy of praxis—is once again a purely theoretical question. Theory accordingly already possesses in principle a primacy over praxis through the fact that the question of whether theory or praxis is primary, and the decision on this issue, come under theory.[30]

Aschenberg does not seem to do justice here to the fact that within *Knowing and Doing* itself Prauss points out that he does *not* see his own inquiry in "purely theoretical" terms. Thus Prauss might well respond to Aschenberg by pointing to those passages in his text where he stresses the practical import of his own inquiry (see, for example, pp. xxiii and 61 below). This dispute between Prauss and Aschenberg goes to the very heart of the question concerning the relationship between theory and practice.

Aschenberg also suggests that the tenets of Prauss's practicism make it impossible to "state the conditions which make the attainment of success and truth possible transcendentally."[31] This is to suggest, as Rohs intimates, that Prauss's practicism does not make it possible to substantiate judgments regarding the validity of noemata; Aschenberg bases this claim on the idea, advanced by Hans Wagner, that "the logical conditions and principles of the truth of noemata cannot at all be made comprehensible" from a phenomenological standpoint such as Prauss's, which conceives knowing exclusively in terms of intentional noesis and poiesis rather than in terms of "the noematic-poiematic content-aspect," which would entail a primacy of theory.[32] If Aschenberg and Wagner are right, Prauss's (and indeed *any*) phenomenological starting point fails to pay respect to the principle that "in the structure of transcendental philosophy the phenomenological reflection on the constitution of contents is subordinate to the logical reflection on the *validity* of contents, which leads back to a transcendental subject being the principle of all validity, i.e., to a *subjectum veritatis.*"[33]

These criticisms and questions do not simply focus the issue of whether and to what extent the goals of transcendental philosophy can be realized through phenomenological method; they also show the depth and significance of the problems with which Prauss has concerned himself. Notwithstanding the challenges that Prauss's critics have raised, the relevance of his emphasis on subjectivity's practical dimension and its "obsession with success" to the status of contemporary technological society cannot be overstated. He has presented us with a subtle and suggestive program for the development of transcendental philosophy into a viable theory of action; and, in a most timely way, he has called us back from a preoccupation with the constitutive noesis-character of Heidegger's thought, and directed us toward the question of the validity of its noematic content.

A Note on the Translation

Much of what follows is an interpretation of Heidegger's *Sein und Zeit*; where Prauss cites that text, we have for the most part followed John Macquarrie and Edward Robinson's translation of *Sein und Zeit* (New York: Harper & Row, 1962), on the theory that it is the most widely used English translation of Heidegger's major work. Prauss's page references to *Sein und Zeit* are to the 11th edition; fortunately, the page numbers given in the margins of the Macquarrie and Robinson translation, as well as those in the margins of Joan Stambaugh's more recent translation (Albany: State University of New York Press, 1996), will coincide with the page numbers of the 11th edition. Thus we hope that readers of our translation will be able to find the relevant passages of Heidegger's major work quickly in whatever version of it they use.

Several German terms Prauss employs present special difficulties in translation. *Handeln*, for example, is a rather awkward word to render in English. It seems best captured by "doing," as this stays closest to a verbal form. Where "doing" seemed inappropriate, however, we replaced it with "activity" or "action" (especially in the essay "Heidegger and Practical Philosophy," where "theory of action" is the accepted philosophical term in English, rather than "theory of doing").

Certain technical terms Heidegger uses also proved problematic, such as *eigentlich*, which in the nominalized form *Eigentlichkeit* is usually translated "authenticity," but which, as an adjective or adverb, often has a more ordinary sense; to express this, we have, for example, either used "really" or "ultimately." The title of Prauss's fifth chapter is a perfect example of the issue here: we have translated *Der eigentliche Primat des Handelns vor dem Erkennen* as "The *Real* Primacy of Doing over Knowing," even though the concept of authenticity might not be out of place here, insofar as Prauss accuses Heidegger of "falling" into an understanding of the environment in terms that are "really" more appropriate to Dasein itself.

Finally, we have translated *Einschlag* as "import"; Prauss uses this term to indicate, for example, that knowing always has a practical impact, upshot, or outcome.

NOTES

1. See, for example, Hans-Georg Gadamer, *Truth and Method*, second rev. ed., trans. Joel Weinsheimer and Donald G. Marshall (New York: Crossroad, 1992), pp. 296–98.
2. Karl Löwith, *Martin Heidegger and European Nihilism*, ed. Richard Wolin, trans. Gary Steiner (New York: Columbia University Press, 1995), p. 34.
3. Gerold Prauss, *Kant über Freiheit als Autonomie* (Frankfurt: Klostermann, 1983).
4. Ibid., p. 12.
5. Ibid., p. 16; cf. pp. 14–15.
6. Ibid., p. 309.
7. Ibid., p. 219.
8. Ibid., pp. 310ff.
9. Ibid., pp. 310, 312.
10. Ibid., p. 312.
11. Prauss does so not only in *Knowing and Doing in Heidegger's "Being and Time,"* "Heidegger and Practical Philosophy," and his discussion of the German Idealists in *Kant über Freiheit als Autonomie*, but also most recently in *Die Welt und wir. Erster Band, Erster Teil: Sprache-Subjekt-Zeit* (Stuttgart/Weimar: Metzler, 1990), pp. 217–40.
12. *Kant über Freiheit als Autonomie*, p. 314.
13. Ibid., p. 315.
14. See "Heidegger and Practical Philosophy," pp. 64ff. below. Reiner Schürmann captures the essential difference between the prospects for a Kantian theory of action and the later Heidegger's retreat from action theory when he points out that "in Kantianism the transcendental apparatus legitimates knowledge and action, whereas the Heideggerian retrieval of originary presencing, twin to the delegitimation of regulations of obedience, produces neither scientific knowledge nor any moral law. Rather, it divests thought of all founding power regarding knowledge and action. Stated positively, it invests thought with a new mandate: that of pointing out the historical unfolding of being-there,

each configuration of which has been produced by its epochal economy." Reiner Schürmann, *Heidegger on Being and Acting: From Principles to Anarchy*, trans. Christine-Marie Gros in collaboration with the author (Bloomington: Indiana University, 1990), p. 157.

15. *Kant über Freiheit als Autonomie*, p. 317.

16. Ibid., p. 322. Prauss also criticizes Hegel for misunderstanding Kant's notion of practical love; see *Kant über Freiheit als Autonomie*, pp. 318ff.

17. *Kant über Freiheit als Autonomie*, p. 323.

18. Ibid., p. 324.

19. Ibid., p. 325.

20. Prauss's own work in this area culminates in *Die Welt und wir*, a work that Prauss has envisaged in two volumes. To date only the first volume, in two parts, has appeared. See *Die Welt und wir. Erster Band, Zweiter Teil: Raum-Substanz-Kausalität* (Stuttgart/Weimar: Metzler, 1993); for information on the first part of vol. one, see note 11 above. Prauss has presented his influential interpretation of Kant not only in *Kant über Freiheit als Autonomie*, but also in *Erscheinung bei Kant. Ein Problem der "Kritik der reinen Vernunft"* (Berlin: De Gruyter, 1971), and *Kant und das Problem der Dinge an Sich* (Bonn: Bouvier, 1974).

21. *Kant über Freiheit als Autonomie*, p. 216n7.

22. Ibid., p. 219; in "Heidegger and Practical Philosophy," Prauss attributes this to Kant: see p. 69 below.

23. Peter Rohs, review of Gerold Prauss, *Erkennen und Handeln in Heideggers "Sein und Zeit,"* *Philosophisches Jahrbuch* 85 (1978): 424–26.

24. See below, p. 31.

25. Rohs review, p. 426.

26. Ibid., p. 426.

27. Reinhold Aschenberg, review of Gerold Prauss, *Erkennen und Handeln in Heideggers "Sein und Zeit,"* Roberto de Amorim Almeida, *Natur und Geschichte. Zur Frage nach der ursprünglichen Dimension abendländischen Denkens vor dem Hintergrund der Auseinandersetzung zwischen Martin Heidegger und Karl Löwith,* and Winfried Franzen, *Von der Existentialontologie zur Seinsgeschichte. Eine Untersuchung über die Entwicklung der Philosophie Martin Heideggers, Philosophy and History* 2 (1978): 154–65, pp. 163f.

28. Aschenberg review, p. 164.

29. See *Being and Time*, section 32, "Understanding and Interpretation"; cf. pp. 186f. for Heidegger's characterization of Dasein's "sight." See also *Logik: Die Frage nach der Wahrheit, Gesamtausgabe,* Vol. 21 (Frankfurt: Klostermann, 1976), pp. 135–61. Of course, Heidegger's discussions of equipmental breakdown and the equipmental use of signs are also of vital importance in this connection; see *Being and Time*, sections 16 and 17.

30. Aschenberg review, p. 164.

31. Ibid., p. 165.

32. Ibid., pp. 164f.; cf. Hans Wagner, *Philosophie und Reflexion* (Munich/Basle: E. Reinhardt, 1959), sections 5–7.

33. Aschenberg review, p. 165.

Reference Note

Paragraph or page numbers without title refer to Martin Heidegger, *Sein und Zeit*, 11th ed. (Tübingen: Max Niemeyer Verlag, 1967).

Introduction

The theme of knowing and doing, or of theory and practice, was discussed thoroughly as the theme of subjectivity by the German Idealists in connection with Kant. But by now it has become apparent that they encountered difficulties regarding just what is fundamental to this theme: Are the knowing and doing of subjectivity (understood as intentionality) perhaps one and the same? Or if not: To what extent are knowing and doing always distinct from each other, as mere kinds of intentionality? Do knowing and doing then stand in a definite relationship to one another as such kinds of intentionality? And if so: In what relationship? They ventured into all these fundamental questions and difficulties further than anyone else, but in the end they were not able to give a convincing answer to any of them.

The reason why this discussion has not continued after them is not at all because they may have completed it. Instead, it breaks off with them solely because no one since them appears able, nor dares, to press on to these fundamental questions, with a single exception: Martin Heidegger. With the "Fundamental Ontology" of *Being and Time*, as a theory of "Dasein," of human subjectivity, he is the only one who ventures to take up these questions again. But here he encounters the same difficulties that the German idealists encountered before him. Hence the danger exists that with Heidegger's *Being and Time* the discussion of these questions will again break off.

But today just as before, not to let it break off is more than a matter of theoretical interest; it is first of all a matter of practical interest. For in both cases this breaking off encourages the disastrously precipitous action of abandoning, solely because of its difficulty, the project of working out the appropriate human understanding of world and self, an understanding which may well be correct but which can be attained only with difficulty. What is left is another understanding, whose simplicity easily obscures its falsity and thus also obscures the fact that it destroys the prospects for a properly oriented future.

1.

The Theory of Concern

Even the following cursory considerations show the extent of the difficulties raised by Heidegger's fundamental questioning. As is well known, Heidegger seeks to get at the unsolved problem of knowing and doing or of theory and practice in human subjectivity by attempting to understand both (not just doing and practice but rather knowing and theory as well) fundamentally as kinds or modes of "concern," which he sets forth as the fundamental characteristic of human "Dasein." Those interpreters who examine this doctrine of concern more closely come up with interpretations that are striking because, on the one hand, they can be substantiated very well by the text of *Being and Time*, while, on the other hand, they nonetheless differ very sharply from one another. Where one view holds that with this doctrine of concern Heidegger wants to show a "primacy of practice over theory,"[1] of doing over knowing, another will instead see in it an attempt to "dissolve" the traditional distinction between knowing and doing or theory and practice generally.[2]

At first glance one will be inclined to hold that these interpretations are incompatible. For only one who fundamentally acknowledges the difference between doing and knowing is capable of demonstrating, in a meaningful way, a primacy of the former over the latter. Likewise, one who has once denied this distinction between doing and knowing can never again reasonably consider proving the primacy of the one over the other. It becomes clear upon closer inspection, though, that not only do these two interpretations not contradict each other, but in fact they even complement each other; most importantly, when taken together they yield a suitable interpretation of Heidegger's doctrine of concern. Only such an interpretation can show that these two essential characteristics of Heidegger's doctrine—the attempted proof of a primacy of practice over theory and the dissolution of their distinction—are internally connected. Exposing this can help us to move beyond a historical interpretation of Heidegger's doctrine and move toward a substantive and systematic insight into the relation between knowing and doing or between theory and practice.

1

That, in any case, Heidegger attempts, in his doctrine of concern, to set forth a primacy of doing and practice over knowing and theory becomes clear from the following consideration alone: he wants to show a primacy of the "readiness-to-hand" of those beings with which humans as concernful Dasein deal, over their mere "presence-at-hand." "The kind of dealing which is [primary or] closest to us is . . . not bare perceptual cognition, but rather that kind of concern which manipulates things and puts them to use . . . such entities are not thereby objects for knowing the 'world' theoretically, they are simply what gets used, what gets produced, and so forth" (p. 67). Hence in contrast with mere "things, which as objects of mere knowing possess solely the mode of being of "presence-at-hand," Heidegger says explicitly: "We shall call those entities which we encounter in concern '*equipment*' . . . the kind of Being which equipment possesses—in which it manifests itself in its own right—we call '*readiness-to-hand*' " (pp. 68f.).

Just how emphatically he advocates with this primacy of the readiness-to-hand of equipment a primacy of human doing and practice as well becomes completely clear from this: according to Heidegger, Dasein can make possible for itself theoretical knowledge of beings as solely present-at-hand things only on the basis of its primarily practical dealing with those beings (which just for that reason are also primarily ready-to-hand equipment), and furthermore this is done only through an alteration of its attitude toward these beings themselves. "If knowing is to be possible as a way of determining the nature of the present-at-hand by observing it, then there must first be a *deficiency* in our having-to-do with the world concernfully. When concern holds back from any kind of producing, manipulating, and the like" or in "holding-itself-back from any manipulation or utilization . . . concern puts itself into what is now the sole remaining mode," namely, into knowing as mere "*perception* of the present-at-hand." Again, "in knowing, Dasein achieves a new *status of being* towards a world which has already been discovered in Dasein itself," that is, toward the world which "*originally*" and "*beforehand*" is always already uncovered in Dasein's practical concern. And "this new possibility of being can develop itself autonomously; it can become a task to be accomplished, and as scientific knowledge it can take over the guidance for Being-in-the-world" (pp. 61f).

But already in this formulation of his thesis regarding the primacy of doing over knowing, Heidegger encounters an initial difficulty.

On the one hand, he actually goes so far with this thesis as to claim that beings are uncovered by Dasein primarily through its *doing* and hence primarily as ready-to-hand equipment. This can be traced to his formulations of the relevant examples: "Hammering itself uncovers the specific manipulability of the hammer," that is, this "equipment" in its specific "readiness-to-hand"; such uncovering, "hammering," for example, "has appropriated this equipment in a way which could not possibly be more suitable" (p. 69).[3] On the other hand, Heidegger himself must acknowledge that in a certain respect he takes this claim too far.

For what does it really mean to say something like "hammering itself uncovers"?

Of course this cannot mean that hammering with a hammer is itself and as such an uncovering, for example, a catching sight of this hammer. It is clear what Heidegger is after here: if in fact there exists a primacy of doing (as dealings with the ready-to-hand) over mere knowing (of the present-at-hand), then the possibility is thereby precluded that such doing could be conditioned by such knowing. But it is clear what this actually amounts to: since even in everyday doing, which Heidegger takes as his point of departure here, knowing must also play a role somehow—for how could hammering with a hammer be possible without uncovering this hammer?—doing and knowing here threaten to collapse into one another, and indeed not just knowing into doing but rather doing into knowing as well.

For Heidegger cannot help admitting, in connection with everyday doing, that "when we deal with [things] by using them and manipulating them, this activity is not a blind one"; according to his own formulation, this means that even doing "has its own kind of sight, by which our manipulation is guided" (p. 69). According to Heidegger this "sight" shows that doing certainly possesses "its own kind of sight," which precisely because of its unique character he calls "circumspection" and conceives as something which as "sight" or "observation" is itself already "primordially a kind of concern" (p. 69).

It is clear what Heidegger is after here: for if in fact there exists a primacy of doing as dealings with the ready-to-hand over mere knowing of the present-at-hand, then the possibility is precluded that such "sight" (which is now a condition for doing) could be a case of knowing the present-at-hand. But what this actually amounts to is clear: since according to Heidegger the very "observation" proper to such "circumspection" is also supposed to be "primordially a kind of concern" (p. 69), then, from the standpoint of knowing, knowing and doing again threaten to collapse into one another under the rubric of "concern." If it seemed before as if something like hammering was itself an uncovering and doing was itself a knowing, conversely it now seems as if uncovering is itself something like hammering and knowing is itself something like doing.

It can be made even clearer that the difficulty that Heidegger encounters here is of a fundamental kind. It does not emerge exclusively in this conception of concern for the ready-to-hand, which together with its specific sighting of the ready-to-hand is supposed to have a primacy over all knowing of the merely present-at-hand.

Rather, it is also a burden for Heidegger's conception of the knowing of the present-at-hand itself, whose purest imprint he sees in natural science.

This becomes clearest in section 69, which is probably the most important section for the theme of "knowing and doing." There, in discussing "the way in which circumspective concern with the ready-to-hand changes over into an exploration of what we come across as present-at-hand within the world," Heidegger attempts to specify what this change-over actually consists in (p. 357), an attempt that manifestly gives him trouble. It becomes clear to him there "that it is by no means obvious where the ontological boundary between 'theoretical' and 'atheoretical' behavior really runs!" (p. 358). This is apparent simply from the fact that here Heidegger sees himself forced to a critique that is not immediately recognizable as a self-critique, since Heidegger does not expressly declare it as such: "In characterizing the change-over from the manipulating and using and so forth which are circumspective in a 'practical' way, to 'theoretical' exploration, it would be easy to suggest that merely looking at entities is something which emerges when concern *holds back* from any kind of manipulation" (p. 357).

But in fact Heidegger himself, as has already been shown, offered just this characterization at the beginning of *Being and Time* (e.g., p. 61). Here, on the other hand, he now lodges a critique against such a conception and hence in the end against himself, since "what is decisive in the 'emergence' of the theoretical attitude would then lie in the *disappearance* of practice" (p. 357). With the mere "discontinuance of a specific manipulation in our concernful dealings," "the circumspection" regarding ready-to-hand equipment "which guides manipulating" does not yet become knowing of merely present-at-hand things; with this "the 'theoretical' attitude of science is by no means yet reached" (pp. 357f.). On the contrary: "Our concern then diverts itself specifically into a just-looking-around," indeed, it can even "take on the character of a more precise kind of circumspection, such as 'inspecting,' checking up on what has been attained, or looking over the 'operations' which are now 'at a standstill.' Holding back from the use of equipment is so far from sheer 'theory' that the kind of circumspection which tarries and 'considers,' remains wholly in the grip of the ready-to-hand equipment with which one is concerned" (p. 357).

The basis for this self-critique is clear: precisely because, according to this conception, not only something like manipulating, but rather also the circumspection itself which guides it, is already supposed to count fundamentally as a kind of concern for the ready-to-hand, it follows that a mere absence of manipulating (which of course always attaches itself first of all to such a guiding circumspection) can fundamentally change nothing about the character of this circumspection as a specific sighting of ready-to-hand equipment.

NOTES

1. Thus, for example, Ernst Tugendhat, *Der Wahrheitsbegriff bei Husserl und Heidegger*, 2nd ed. (Berlin: De Gruyter, 1970), p. 288; cf. also Walter Bröcker, "Heidegger und die Logik," in *Heidegger: Perspektiven zur Deutung seines Werks*, 2nd ed., ed. Otto Pöggeler (Köln/Berlin: Kiepenheuer and Witsch, 1970), p. 301; and Otto Friedrich Bollnow, *Philosophie der Erkenntnis* (Stuttgart: Kohlhammer, 1970), pp. 44f.

2. Thus for example Pöggeler, "Einleitung: Heidegger Heute," in *Heidegger*, p. 34.

3. Cf. also p. 67, where it is stated that these beings as ready-to-hand equipment are "encountered of their own accord *in* our concern with them."

2.

The Alleged Primacy of Doing over Knowing

It has become apparent that according to Heidegger circumspection must in itself already count as a kind of concern. But then conversely the same counts for the knowing of present-at-hand things as well: whatever that "change-over" of circumspection as a specific sighting of the ready-to-hand into the mere knowing of the present-at-hand may consist in—putting aside for the moment an examination of it—even this knowing of merely present-at-hand things, especially as it unfolds into the natural sciences, must itself according to this conception count fundamentally as a kind of concern (cf., e.g., pp. 56f., 193, 351) and hence must itself also have some kind of practical import. Therefore, it is not at all surprising when Heidegger says explicitly in this connection that "just as practice has its own specific kind of sight," that is, just as the manipulation of ready-to-hand equipment is subject to the guidance of circumspection regarding ready-to-hand equipment, so too "theoretical research," natural science as knowledge of present-at-hand things, "is not without a practice of its own" (p. 358).

Understanding what this means is made easier given what Heidegger himself says. According to him, to the extent that natural science always already aims ultimately at a practice of its own, namely, at technology, it is obvious that even natural science has its own kind of practice and, hence, has, as theory, practical import. Such *knowledge* of nature stands in the service of the *mastery* of nature from the start, serving to encroach upon nature in accordance with the knowledge of its laws, not simply letting it run its course but rather steering it according to human will: "Because physics, indeed already as pure theory, sets nature up to exhibit itself as a coherence of forces calculable in advance,"[1] it is therefore the case that "modern science as theory . . . is a refining of the real that does encroach uncannily upon it"[2] and which at bottom then simply develops into (*sich . . . fortsetzt*) technology. Hence, according to Heidegger, to speak as if the practice of technology first emerges as something like "applied natural science" is to create a "deceptive appearance."[3]

But then our surprise is that much greater when, after Heidegger's claim that even this "theoretical research is not without a practice of its own," we read further in *Being and Time* and encounter the following examples in support of this claim: "Reading off the measurements which result from an experiment often requires a complicated 'technical' set-up for the experimental design. Observation with a microscope is dependent upon the production of 'preparations' " (p. 358). In the one place where Heidegger mentions technology (*Technik*) at all in *Being and Time*, only the adjective "technical" (*technisch*) appears, and even this appears only in quotation marks; in the one place where Heidegger comes to speak of something like technology at all in *Being and Time*, by no means does he have in mind the *practice* of the mastery of nature, which unfolds *from out of* knowledge of nature into the uncanny— rather, he has in mind only what is comparatively harmless in those "technologies" which natural scientific research employs *for* the production of its *own theories*.

Our surprise about this is so great that at first we cannot believe that this is at all possible for Heidegger. Indeed, no matter how precisely one re-reads for this, one does not find a single place in *Being and Time* where Heidegger went beyond these mere "technologies" (which of course are "practical" only as the *means* of natural scientific *theory*) and presented *technology* as the *purpose* of, and hence as that which is *authentically practical* in, natural science.

On the contrary, such a re-reading gives rise to an additional surprise: it is not simply the case that these "technologies" are all that Heidegger designates as the practical import of theoretical knowing in *Being and Time*, and that such designation there enables him when necessary to conceive natural science as the distinctive case of knowledge of the present-at-hand and yet also as a case of concern; these "technologies" are all that Heidegger *can* designate in *Being and Time* as such practical import. For apart from this talk of the practical import of theoretical knowing, he conceives the mere knowledge of the present-at-hand and thus natural science itself in every respect as a case of pure θεωρία in Aristotle's sense:[4] as a case in which theory, to the extent that it is still purposive, is its own purpose. As the distinctive case of knowing the present-at-hand, Heidegger characterizes natural science over and over in *Being and Time* as a "quiet tarrying alongside" or "pure perception of" the present-at-hand, in which Dasein no longer pursues any purposes at all (whereas it does in circumspection regarding the ready-to-hand), that is, in which Dasein does not at all aim at practice and especially not at technology.[5]

Thus one has misunderstood the substantive and systematic position of *Being and Time* from the ground up if one maintains about it, as for example Walter Bröcker already has, that "the present-at-hand is the correlate of theoretical examination, whose methodologically matured and systematic form is modern science. *Its essence, according to Heidegger, is technology*."[6] On the contrary, there can be no talk whatsoever of the latter in *Being and Time*. For if Heidegger were already to advocate this in *Being and Time*, then he could in no way understand natural science there as the "methodologically matured and systematic form of the theoretical examination of the present-at-hand," as he in fact does; rather, he would then have to conceive it as the "methodologically matured and systematic form of practical circumspection regarding the ready-to-hand."

This all the more as Heidegger in *Being and Time* ascribes "reckoning" or "calculative" thinking, which Bröcker sees in natural science as knowledge of the present-at-hand, instead to circumspective dealings with the ready-to-hand.[7] As a science "whose essence is technology," as a theory "whose essence is practice," natural science simply would not be the distinctive case of the mere knowledge of present-at-hand things, but would instead be a distinctive case of circumspection regarding ready-to-hand equipment.

But the insight into this practical-technological character of natural science itself is not yet present in *Being and Time* and cannot yet be present there at all. For with his conception of natural science as the distinctive case of knowledge of merely present-at-hand things, which in the sense of Aristotelian θεωρία emerges only to the extent that Dasein steps out of practical circumspection regarding ready-to-hand equipment,[8] Heidegger occupies an entirely different standpoint.

This insight does not appear in *Being and Time* itself and hence does not obviously undermine his position there, but instead appears only after *Being and Time* as a simple revision of that position; this revision appears so inconspicuously that it receives little attention. People are apparently so fixated on the "turning" that Heidegger supposedly made only after *Being and Time* that they lose sight of the fact that with this insight Heidegger actually makes a shift after *Being and Time* that is more significant in a substantive and systematic respect than his "turning," because it is more fundamental.

This insight means nothing less than that the conception of knowing and doing and their relationship, and accordingly the conception in *Being and Time* of the relationship between the present-at-hand and the ready-to-hand as well, cannot be maintained. Precisely this knowing of the present-at-hand, which in *Being and Time* is supposed to emerge as pure θεωρία through a change-over from circumspection regarding the ready-to-hand, must instead have a practical import from the start, insofar as it is something that simply develops into natural science and technology from out of circumspection. Thus it cannot be distinct from circumspection. Conversely, this means that even in circumspective dealings with the ready-to-hand, knowing the present-at-hand must already play an essential role, for in principle such dealings simply unfold further into natural science and technology.

With this we are again confronted with the task of determining exactly what the essence of knowing and doing consists in, and in what relationship they really stand to one another. But Heidegger no longer endeavors to solve this new problem. For the more he acknowledges this insight, the more he evaluates it negatively. And from this we can at least roughly estimate how distressing it might have been for Heidegger to have to realize that technology itself, which he increasingly comes to see as the greatest danger for humanity, is already tied up with that relationship of humanity to beings which he considers primordial in *Being and Time*, namely, circumspective dealings with the ready-to-hand.

Thus this insight does not lead to the articulation of a correspondingly new, revised theory of the knowing and doing of Dasein; Heidegger can now see in it only the beginning of the end, the origin of that "subjectivity of the subject" which in technology finally upends itself completely.[9] Instead this insight forms the authentic ground for the "turning," that is, for Heidegger's attempt in a countermove to develop out of *Being and Time* just those foundations which will let him argue for something in human beings that bestows on them their authentic essence prior to their knowing and doing, and more primordially than either.

In order to help express this essence adequately, he wrestled right up to the end with the possibilities of language. However he may understand this essence as a whole, he clearly ascribes to it the features of θεωρία. But by this he no longer means the mere knowing of the present-at-hand which was supposed to be subordinated to circumspective activity [*Handeln*] regarding the ready-to-hand; rather he means here a θεωρία that is ordered fundamentally prior to both knowing and doing [*Handeln*].[10]

In view of this later conception of human beings, it ought to be of substantive and systematic interest for philosophy to develop the earlier conception completely, and indeed all the more as Heidegger continually contrasts this later conception with that earlier one, which he himself leaves undeveloped. In exactly what does the full subjectivity of the subject really consist—the subjectivity that for Heidegger follows from the revision of the untenable theory of knowing and doing in *Being and Time*?

NOTES

1. Martin Heidegger, "Die Frage nach der Technik," *Vorträge und Aufsätze*, 4th ed. (Pfullingen: Neske, 1978), p. 25 [*Translators' note*. Here and in what follows we have used existing English translations

of Heidegger's essays where possible. The translation of this passage is by William Lovitt, from "The Question Concerning Technology," in *The Question Concerning Technology and Other Essays* (New York: Harper & Row, 1977), which will be cited below as QCT; the passage quoted above is found on p. 21.]

2. Ibid., p. 52. ["Science and Reflection," QCT, p. 167.]

3. Cf. ibid., p. 27. ["The Question Concerning Technology," QCT, p. 23.]

4. Cf. e.g., *Sein und Zeit*, p. 138, and *Vorträge und Aufsätze*, pp. 48f. ["Science and Reflection," QCT, pp. 163f.]

5. Cf., e.g., pp. 25f., 33, 61f., 138, 158, 170ff., 357ff., further ¶21.

6. Walter Bröcker, "Heidegger und die Logik," in *Philosophische Rundschau* 1 (1953–54); now in Heidegger: *Perspektiven zur Deutung seines Werks*, 2nd ed., ed. Otto Pöggeler (Köln/Berlin: Kiepenheuer and Witsch, 1970), p. 301 (emphasis mine).

7. Cf., e.g., pp. 111f., 289, 292, 294, 324.

8. Cf. p. 69: "Theoretical behavior is just looking, without circumspection."

9. Cf. "Vom Wesen des Grundes," *Wegmarken*, 2nd ed. (Frankfurt: Klostermann, 1978), pp. 159f. [*The Essence of Reasons*, bilingual ed., trans. Terence Malick (Evanston: Northwestern University Press, 1969), pp. 97–99] and also, e.g., particularly *Vorträge und Aufsätze*, pp. 73, 176 ["The Thing," in *Poetry, Language, Thought*, trans. Albert Hofstadter (New York: Harper Colophon, 1971), pp. 185f.], and also pp. 51ff. ["Science and Reflection," QCT, pp. 166ff.], pp. 82ff., pp. 109f. ["Who is Nietzsche's Zarathustra?" in *The New Nietzsche*, ed. David B. Allison (Cambridge: MIT Press, 1986), pp. 71f.], and p. 124 ["What Calls for Thinking?" in *Basic Writings*, rev. ed., ed. David Farrell Krell (San Francisco: Harper and Row, 1993), p. 372].

10. Cf., e.g., *Vorträge und Aufsätze*, pp. 163 ["The Thing," *Poetry, Language, Thought*, pp. 172f.], 174 [ibid., pp. 183f.], and cf. also pp. 51ff. below.

3.

The Primacy of Knowing over Doing

It has been shown that in his theory of concern in *Being and Time* Heidegger must attempt to show that even theoretical knowing has a specific practical import, and that theoretical knowing itself is in principle an instance of concern. At the same time, in this theory he also aims at a primacy of practice over theory. Thus he is able to establish that there is something like a practical import for this theoretical knowing of the present-at-hand (which is supposed to emerge first of all through a "change-over" from practical dealings with the ready-to-hand) only by appealing to those "technologies" of which this knowing, particularly as natural science, avails itself: that which is authentically practical in this science, namely, its tendency toward technology, was not uncovered by Heidegger at this time but only later. But if historically speaking there is something surprising in this, substantively and systematically it amounts to something almost grotesque.

For in his theory of concern Heidegger finds it necessary to establish that there is a practical import in theory itself only because he is compelled to hold fundamentally to a kind of parallel between theoretical knowing of the present-at-hand and practical dealings with the ready-to-hand, since in principle both are supposed to be concern. He himself articulates this parallel explicitly when he says, in a passage already cited: "Just as praxis has its own specific kind of sight . . . theoretical research is not without a praxis of its own" (p. 358). In connection with this parallel, Heidegger then designates particular "technologies" as the practical import of theory—for example, observations through a microscope—which would in turn have to mean that even the "sight" or "circumspection" of "practice" possesses its specifically practical aspect only insofar as everyday Dasein likewise avails itself of such "technologies," for example, insofar as it wears glasses.

Surely Heidegger does not mean anything like this when he posits circumspection regarding the ready-to-hand as a specifically practical knowing, as a "knowing" that is as such itself directed toward dealings, as a "theory" that is as such itself directed toward practice. But there is also no doubt that it is precisely here that for

13

the first time it becomes questionable, in *Being and Time* itself, whether there is in fact, as Heidegger claims, a difference between practical circumspection regarding the ready-to-hand and theoretical knowing of the present-at-hand.

For from the fact that Heidegger overlooks what is authentically practical in natural science as knowledge of the present-at-hand (namely, that knowing itself is directed toward doing, and theory itself toward practice) and sees it only in circumspection regarding the ready-to-hand, it is apparent that Heidegger would like not only to conceive the knowing of the present-at-hand as something *purely* theoretical (θεωρία), but also to conceive circumspection regarding the ready-to-hand as something *purely* practical. Should this theoretical knowing of present-at-hand things— leaving aside particular "technologies"—as such be something that is in no sense practical, then by the same token that practical circumspection regarding ready-to-hand equipment would also be nothing at all theoretical and in no sense a knowing of present-at-hand things.

Since, however, the former as Heidegger understands it has already become questionable, the latter must in the same sense also become questionable. From the former it becomes clear that the theoretical and the practical *cannot* be so neatly divided into fundamentally different kinds of knowing, as Heidegger has in mind with his strict distinction between purely practical circumspection regarding ready-to-hand equipment and purely theoretical knowing of present-at-hand things. If in the case of natural science the theoretical can accompany the practical in the sense indicated, then by the same token in the case of circumspection the practical would have to be able to accompany the theoretical. But this would mean that knowledge of present-at-hand things and circumspection regarding ready-to-hand equipment would ultimately have to coincide, since each would be both theoretical and practical in precisely the same sense.

That this coinciding of the theoretical and the practical would have to count for circumspection can be made quite convincing when it is shown not merely by being deduced from natural science as the distinctive case of knowledge of the present-at-hand, but rather by also being shown independently of this, in circumspection regarding the ready-to-hand itself. That is, we are confronted here with the task of investigating more closely whether it is really so imperative to conceive of circumspection (as Heidegger does) as purely practical knowing of the ready-to-hand, and thereby to deny any import of theoretical knowledge of the present-at-hand to circumspection.

In particular, it must be recognized that Heidegger cannot help letting circumspection regarding the ready-to-hand count at the very least as a perception of the ready-to-hand. Not only does this become clear implicitly in expressions like "circumspection" (*Umsicht*) or "sight" (*Sichten*), which without a doubt intend a seeing of the ready-to-hand (p. 149); but Heidegger also expresses this explicitly when he says, for example, that circumspection appears not only as seeing but rather also as hearing (pp. 163f.). And something like "circumspective hearing" does not signify a substantive paradox at all, but at most a linguistic one, since it means only that circumspection appears fundamentally as perception, or alternatively that perception itself possesses from the beginning that practical import which is what primarily makes it circumspection (cf. the bottom of p. 149).

But this then presents the question of how it is at all possible for Heidegger to attribute to such circumspective perception an *exclusively* practical character and to deny of it any of the theoretical character of a knowledge of the present-at-hand. From the notion of perception as circumspection it must necessarily follow for Heidegger that such perception does not in any case amount to perceiving *something*, but rather consists fundamentally in perceiving something *as something*—and that means perceiving [something] *as something determinate*. Therefore, Heidegger cannot help but say that "in dealing with what is environmentally ready-to-hand by interpreting it circumspectively," such beings are always seen for example "*as* a table, a door, a carriage, or a bridge," and that such seeing accordingly always already has the full structure of the "something as something" or the "as-structure" as well (p. 149).

But that such perceiving constantly appears as a perceiving of something as something would then also have to mean that even this perceiving itself is already to be conceived in the full sense as an "observing" or a "determining" of something as something, and thus precisely as a knowing of the present-at-hand, which Heidegger himself continually designates as "determining . . . by observing" (p. 61). Heidegger is able to avert this consequence only by means of a doctrine which, taken by itself, is hardly convincing, and which in the context of *Being and Time* actually leads to an inconsistency. Heidegger is able to deny that circumspective perception has the character of this determining and thus the character of knowing the present-at-hand only by claiming that such perceiving, in spite of its "structure of something as something," consists solely in a "pre-predicative understanding" (p. 359) and is solely a "mere pre-predicative seeing of the ready-to-hand" (p. 149); whereas "determining" as "predication" befits only the "assertion which characterizes determinately" (p. 149, cf. p. 359).

This idea of a "pre-predicative" perception remains unclear, however, and indeed it remains so in two ways. Not only does it not become clear what this structure of the "something as something"—which even Heidegger must grant to perception— is to be if it is really different from the fundamental structure of predication; at the same time, it also does not become clear how this fundamental structure of predication could consist merely in the outward form of an assertion.

Taken together, all of this amounts to the following: How could such predication ever constitute the explicit structure of an "assertion which characterizes determinately" as the structure of an articulated perception, if such perception did not also possess just this predicative structure even when this structure is unarticulated and unspoken—that is to say, if it did not also possess this predicative structure implicitly? To say nothing of the fact that in the position that Heidegger is after, it cannot become at all clear how a mere transition to "assertion which characterizes determinately" could by itself take us from circumspection regarding the ready-to-hand to knowledge of the present-at-hand, since for Heidegger these are supposed to be so fundamentally different. Even differences in the content of what is said in such cases, for example, differences between assertions like "the hammer is heavy" and "the hammer is too heavy" or even "too heavy—the other hammer!" are in principle able to change nothing about predicative structure, which is latent even in an extreme abbreviation like "too heavy. . ." (cf. pp. 154, 157).

Indeed, this idea of a perceiving that is still "pre-predicative," and which as such is not yet a knowing of the present-at-hand, leads even further to an inconsistency in the position of *Being and Time* itself. In the fact that Dasein "projects itself towards its potentiality-for-Being in the 'truth'" (p. 363), Heidegger sees one of the reasons for that "change-over" through which human Dasein in each case is first of all supposed to pass from circumspection regarding the ready-to-hand to knowledge of the present-at-hand. Considered by itself, it also becomes immediately clear that with knowledge of the present-at-hand, which has its fundamental structure in predication and its fully elaborated and systematic form in natural science, there in fact emerges in each case something which can be true or in which Dasein can be "in the truth"—something which nonetheless can also be false or in which Dasein can also be "in falsehood." If one adds to this the fact that knowledge of the present-at-hand (and this means predication as something true or false) is always supposed to emerge only through the change-over from circumspection regarding the ready-to-hand, then one encounters interpretive difficulties.

For Heidegger's claim, that circumspection regarding the ready-to-hand is not yet knowledge of the present-at-hand which determines through predication, would then have to mean that circumspection is not yet something that can become true or false. But this absolutely contradicts another of Heidegger's claims in *Being and Time*. It is true that the possibility of falsity in knowing the present-at-hand, which results from that "potentiality-for-Being in the truth" as its opposite, is not expressly mentioned by Heidegger at this point. And yet elsewhere he explicitly formulates this possibility of falsity in circumspection, from which the possibility of truth in circumspection also stems. That is to say, Heidegger definitely sees that even circumspection can "go wrong" or be subject to "delusion," and thus that circumspective perception can also occur as a perceptual error (p. 138).

Now, with this it is conceded that even circumspection emerges fundamentally as something that can become true or false. But how could this be at all possible, unless circumspection itself consisted fundamentally in determining or predicating something as something and hence in knowing the present-at-hand? This is entirely independent of whether or not circumspection as such gets articulated explicitly in a corresponding assertion, since such perceptual error is found even in an unarticulated perception which does not involve any asserting.

On more careful examination it becomes clear that this circumspective perception itself, insofar as it is true or false circumspection regarding the ready-to-hand, must *also* be knowledge of the present-at-hand. But with this, the primacy of doing and practice over knowing and theory that Heidegger is after only becomes more questionable.

For as emphatically as he tries to secure a primacy of practical dealings with the ready-to-hand over knowing the present-at-hand, he must still concede that such dealings proceed not blindly but rather under the direction of circumspection. But with this he is at least conceding a primacy of circumspection over such dealings— though for him there is no such primacy, since he conceives both as something practical and hence ascribes to both, taken together as practice, primacy over knowledge of the present-at-hand as theory.

But if circumspection regarding the ready-to-hand as something true or false is now *also* knowledge of the present-at-hand, then the relationship between theory and practice immediately gets inverted: not only does a primacy of theory over practice arise immediately from the primacy that Heidegger himself must concede to circumspection over dealings (but which he nonetheless thinks he can neglect when considered merely within practice itself, as only a supposed primacy); it also immediately becomes questionable to what extent a subordination of theory to practice (such as Heidegger is attempting) is still to be possible at all.

And in fact, Heidegger encounters still further fundamental difficulties in this attempt, quite independently of the difficulty presented by this purely practical conception of circumspection. But these difficulties are deeper and hence they become conspicuous only once we have already become critical of Heidegger's endeavor.

Thus within his theory of concern (i.e., in terms of his conception of the primacy of doing over knowing) Heidegger presents a series of examples of "concern." The examples are the following: "having to do with something, producing something, attending to something and looking after it, making use of something, giving something up and letting it go, undertaking, accomplishing, evincing, interrogating, considering, discussing, determining . . ." (pp. 56f.). If one bears in mind here that according to Heidegger knowing the present-at-hand consists in "considering" or "determining" the present-at-hand, which is supposed to take place in "assertions" about the present-at-hand that determine it, then at first one sees only that the succession of examples in this series, at least at one point, is not accidental. Instead, the appearance of "considering," "discussing," and "determining" in this series is supposed to show once again that even knowing the present-at-hand is fundamentally an instance of concern; and their appearance only near the end is supposed to indicate in addition that this knowing first emerges as concern, and that it increasingly "refrains" from producing, manipulating, and so on.

Immediately following this Heidegger offers an important addition to the series by saying that "even the deficient modes" of the enumerated examples of concern[1] are themselves "ways of concern," so that among these "deficient modes" he understands the respective "modes of leaving undone" to be included (p. 57). At first there is nothing particularly striking in this. Since in giving examples of this concern Heidegger gives priority to what one traditionally tends to call doing (*Handeln*), this is understandable without further consideration because taking action (*Tun*) and letting be (*Lassen*) are in fact traditionally understood as doing.

Surely it must be recognized that there is a considerable incongruity between these two lists: as "deficient modes" corresponding to the first series of examples, Heidegger gives the examples of "omitting, neglecting, renouncing, taking a rest," a second series which is much shorter than the first. At first this remains inconspicuous, however, since it gives the impression that one really need only allude to such "deficient modes" in order to ensure that for all the examples in the first series there are in fact also examples in the second, which are related to those in the first in the same way that letting be is related to taking action.

It is only when one actually attempts to find such examples that it becomes conspicuous that they exist only for those cases in the first series that are examples of doing and not for those cases that are examples of knowing. For in fact, the omission of an action is itself still an action, while, on the other hand, the omission of a cognition—whatever Heidegger might understand by this—is itself by no means a cognition. And here it is proved for the first time that it is impossible in principle to place knowing and doing together in a series under the rubric of "concern." For the feature just noted, that even the omission of concern is itself still an instance of concern, applies not to knowing but only to doing. This must count as the first indication that in principle knowing itself cannot be conceived as a kind of concern, precisely because for Heidegger doing is the only thing that really falls under the rubric of concern.

This becomes even more apparent from additional characterizations of concern that Heidegger gives only later in *Being and Time*. Thus he says, for example, that concern consists in "'Being directed towards' something possible," yet precisely in the sense that it is "concerning ourselves with something's actualization." For "in concernfully Being directed towards something possible, there is a tendency to *annihilate the possibility* of the possible," precisely because it is directed toward the "actualization" of the possibility and hence toward its "annihilation" as a possibility.

What Heidegger means by this becomes clear when he specifies "producing" something as the primary example of the "concernful actualization of equipment which is ready-to-hand" (p. 261). If one tries, for example, to make a plate out of wood, one is indeed directed toward something possible inasmuch as a plate is in fact something possible when viewed in relation to the wood. But in doing so one is directed toward this possible thing precisely in the sense that one is attempting to actualize it and thereby to annihilate it as a possibility. For one can no longer speak of the plate as a possible thing with respect to the plate that has been produced, while one can speak this way with respect to the [unworked] wood.

Hence Heidegger characterizes concern here quite generally as an intention to change beings, and indeed in the all-encompassing sense in which concern is fundamentally directed toward change not only as the production of something that is not yet actual, but also, for example, as the preservation of something that is already actual.[2] Thus such concern can in general be understood only on the presupposition that in each case that toward which it is directed (e.g., the plate) counts fundamentally as something not yet actual; that is why it seeks in particular to change that from which it proceeds (e.g., the wood), which counts fundamentally as something actual. Accordingly an attempt at such change would be a fundamentally unintelligible instance of concern if it proceeded toward the actualization of something that already counted as actual.

But from this it is apparent that even this characterization of concern applies exclusively to doing and by no means to knowing. Just as certainly as it is correct to say of both knowing and doing that they are always "directed toward something" and hence are intentions toward something, it is equally certain that precisely as such intentions they are nonetheless always specifically distinct from each other as well. That is, if doing is really directed toward something not yet actual, precisely in order to actualize it (plate), and hence on something already actual only in order to change it (wood), then, on the other hand, knowing is oriented genuinely and exclusively toward reaching the actual itself and as such.

Knowing would become a perversion of its ownmost essence if by means of its own intention it were oriented toward changing the actual, its object. We call "knowledge" just that intention which aims at what is, while on the other hand we designate as "action" just that intention which aims at what is not. In any case this must be the minimal definition of that which intends an action as opposed to a cognition. For all further definition—for example, that an action aims at something that is supposed to be—always already presupposes this minimal definition.

Once this has been made clear, one will no longer find it surprising that Heidegger has trouble showing what the change-over really consists in, through which merely theoretical knowing of the present-at-hand is supposed to emerge from circumspective concern for the ready-to-hand. Surely now one will be able to say straightaway that such a plan can never succeed, since in it Heidegger understands knowing fundamentally as concern while at the same time he understands concern fundamentally as doing.

This shows up clearly in section 69 and more particularly in subsection (b), which Heidegger explicitly dedicates to this plan. This entire section is part of his attempt to make the structure of circumspective concern intelligible on the basis of temporal structures. Here too the first thing to become clear is that Heidegger understands concern exclusively in terms of doing, as the intention to change beings. For here he sees the essential feature of its structure in the fact that it forms a kind of intention which, in its temporal aspect, is (as Heidegger expresses it) at once a "making present" and an "awaiting"—which is to say that it is directed as much toward the present as toward the future. In fact this applies to doing as well: as the intention to change beings, for example, to make a plate out of wood, it is related to the present as a relation to wood that is already actual, and it is at the same time related to the future as a relation to the plate that is not yet actual. This means that part of such concern, insofar as it is doing, is the intention to make a being (wood) present in such a way that it at the same time "awaits" something else (the plate) (cf. pp. 352ff.).

This basic definition of concern now constitutes the framework in which Heidegger attempts to show what the "change-over" of circumspection regarding ready-to-hand equipment into the knowing of present-at-hand things consists in. This change-over, which would then in principle also be the origin of natural science as the distinctive case of knowing the present-at-hand, is supposed to take place according to Heidegger as a "thematization" of beings which "objectifies" them. Such "Being which Objectifies and which is alongside the present-at-hand within-the-world" is itself also supposed to be "characterized by a . . . making-present," which is why Heidegger must also immediately add that it is "characterized by a *dis*-

tinctive kind of making-present" (p. 363), for, of course, circumspective concern itself already contains a "making-present." Accordingly there can be a difference between these only on account of what is supposed to be "distinctive" in this latter making-present when compared with the former one.

But Heidegger now adds to this that knowledge of the present-at-hand, and along with it science as a "distinctive kind of making-present," differs "from the Present of circumspection" (more precisely this would have to mean: from the making-present of circumspection) "in that—and above all—the kind of discovering which belongs to the science in question awaits solely the discoveredness of the present-at-hand." Heidegger again explicitly repeats that this knowledge, and along with it science, emerges as the "awaiting of discoveredness . . . of the present-at-hand," in which Dasein "projects itself towards its potentiality-for-Being in the 'truth' " (p. 363).

However, this characterization remains utterly unintelligible, precisely with respect to what Heidegger is attempting to make intelligible by means of it: namely, that and how knowledge of the present-at-hand always emerges first of all from our of circumspection regarding the ready-to-hand. In any event it becomes intelligible when considered with respect to the predicament Heidegger has created for himself, which serves as the basis for his making this attempt.

Since even this knowing is supposed to be fundamentally an instance of concern, it is evident that Heidegger must attempt to demonstrate that along with "making-present" as an essential characteristic of concern, there is within this knowing an "awaiting" as well. It is equally evident that he cannot speak about a primordial discovering with respect to this knowing but rather must proceed from an already existing "discoveredness," since it is precisely circumspection itself which is primordially discovering. But then it must remain simply unintelligible what it would really mean to be still only "awaiting" an already existing "discoveredness" of something, and how it can be at all possible to direct an "awaiting" toward something that is already "in the present."

What is unintelligible in principle in this attempt would even come to light explicitly if Heidegger were to remain faithful to the conception of circumspective concern within it. The already existing "discoveredness" of beings from which he must proceed here is none other than the primordial discoveredness of the *ready-to-hand* in *circumspection*. But then his claim that "discovering" as knowing the present-at-hand and with it "the kind of discovering which belongs to the science in question" consist in "awaiting" this "discoveredness" would in fact have to mean something patently unintelligible: that knowing as the discovering of the *present-at-hand* emerges as "awaiting the discoveredness of the *ready-to-hand*."

And in fact Heidegger is able to avoid being unintelligible here only because at the point of saying what he really has to, he suddenly says something completely different instead: rather than speaking of this "discoveredness" as a "discoveredness of the *ready-to-hand*," he suddenly speaks of it instead as a "discoveredness of the *present-at-hand*," and this means that he attempts to conceive of the emergence of the knowing of the present-at-hand as an "awaiting of the discoveredness of the *present-at-hand*" (p. 363).

Not only, however, does this amount to a pure tautology; primarily it means that here Heidegger himself has lost faith in his position, according to which the primordial discoveredness of beings is fundamentally discoveredness of ready-to-hand equipment:[3] Heidegger is so far from being able to derive something like knowing the present-at-hand originally from circumspective concern, that in the end he must instead presuppose it in that circumspection itself.

Given this, Heidegger's attempt to set forth a primacy of doing and practice over knowing and theory as part of his doctrine of concern must finally be seen as a failure. From the character of this failure it is also apparent that the two interpretations of Heidegger—that Heidegger attempts to show a primacy of practice over theory (Tugendhat), and that he attempts to dissolve the traditional distinction between theory and practice generally (Pöggeler)—not only do not contradict one another, but instead even stand in an inner connection. Only on the condition that Heidegger succeeds in demonstrating this primacy of practice over theory would it be a contradiction for him at the same time to deny the distinction between them. But since he does not succeed in this, the condition for the contradiction is *not* satisfied.

Thus instead of a contradiction the following relation obtains. The attempt to show a primacy of practice over theory fails precisely because in the end it can amount only to the dissolution of the distinction between them; this dissolution, since it is the result of that very attempt, is thus at the same time the sign of its failure. Precisely because such an attempt (to derive something like theory from practice under the rubric of "concern" and hence according to a supposed primacy of practice) can lead only to dissolving theory into practice, in this attempt Heidegger can ultimately preserve something like theory in general only by ordering theory prior to practice, against his real intention. Hence an attempt to demonstrate a primacy of practice over theory, if consistently carried out, *itself* amounts *as such* to an acknowledgment of a primacy of theory over practice instead.

NOTES

1. On the problem of the "deficient mode" in Heidegger, cf. Klaus Hartmann, "The Logic of Deficient and Eminent Modes in Heidegger," *Journal of the British Society for Phenomenology* 5, No. 2 (1974): 118—34.
2. Even as the preservation of something, concern is fundamentally an intention to change something, in this case to change that which threatens the thing to be preserved.
3. And in accordance with this position Heidegger again and again explicitly rejects the idea that beings could primordially "be understood and discovered beforehand as something purely present-at-hand" (p. 71).

4.

The Theory of "Disturbed" Concern

By now it has become clear that Heidegger must concede, contrary to his own intention, a primacy to theory over practice. From this the following conclusion seems to suggest itself: because Heidegger ultimately cannot help acknowledging circumspection regarding ready-to-hand equipment as a knowing of present-at-hand things, what he has in mind in his theory of circumspection can no longer be maintained either. To draw this conclusion, however, would be a mistake. From the fact that Heidegger fails to distinguish knowledge of the present-at-hand from circumspection regarding ready-to-hand equipment, it cannot be concluded that such knowledge is simply a pure knowledge of the present-at-hand completely lacking in circumspection regarding the ready-to-hand. This failure also means that Heidegger does not succeed in demonstrating a "change-over" from circumspection, and hence does not succeed in showing that the knowledge that emerges purely through this "change-over" has the character of mere knowledge of the present-at-hand.

Accordingly he really fails to exhibit two things, namely, a pure circumspection regarding the ready-to-hand which is still not knowledge of the present-at-hand, and a pure knowledge of the present-at-hand which would no longer be circumspection regarding the ready-to-hand. Hence from this failure it would really have to follow that beings are equiprimordially "discovered" by a primordial knowledge both as present-at-hand and as ready-to-hand; this knowledge itself is equiprimordially knowledge of present-at-hand things and circumspection regarding ready-to-hand equipment, and through it the present-at-hand itself is primordially "discovered" as ready-to-hand.

Yet with this Heidegger's basic position would not be invalidated, but would instead survive to the extent that its revision would lead to a result uniting and hence fundamentally preserving these basic ideas of the present-at-hand and the ready-to-hand. And the change in his basic position resulting from this revision would have to be of even greater systematic significance given that it is required, so to speak, by the matter itself. This will all be confirmed through a further examination of Heidegger's theory of concern.

As already mentioned, among other things this theory is characterized by the fact that it takes into account even the "deficient modes" of concern, and hence (to put it briefly) that it treats concern not only positively but negatively as well. And as already mentioned, Heidegger designates as "deficient modes" those negative instances of concern that are related to the corresponding positive instances just as letting be is related to taking action. This is one indication that he understands concern in principle only as doing, because only the omission of an action is itself an action, while in contrast the omission of a cognition is not itself a cognition.

If we bear this in mind, then we can easily see as well that Heidegger does *not* employ the term "deficient mode" univocally with respect to concern.

Instead he specifies other instances of "deficient modes" that are negative instances of concern in a fundamentally different sense than omissions are. This becomes clear in ¶16, which is especially important for his theory because at one point Heidegger comes to speak of instances in which circumspective concern "is disturbed" or is subject to "a disturbance." What "disturbs" here according to Heidegger is fundamentally the ready-to-hand equipment itself. He gives the following examples of this: circumspective concern can be "disturbed" by equipment that is "damaged" or "stands in the way" or is simply "missing" and hence "missed" (cf. pp. 73f.). As Heidegger himself says explicitly, for him such "disturbed" concern always counts equally "as a deficient mode of concern" (p. 73).

If one looks into this more closely, however, it becomes problematic. To what extent is it justified here to use the expression "deficient mode" for these instances as well, when it was first used for instances of omission? It does indeed seem justified to the extent that even the delineated instances of "disturbed" concern ultimately amount to leaving something undone. But here precisely those instances are at issue in which something is left undone solely on account of a "disturbance," something which in the absence of a "disturbance" would by no means be left undone but would instead have been done.

But in its first use the expression "deficient mode" was not meant in this sense at all—as an omission on account of a "disturbance"—but rather in the entirely neutral sense that even wholly undisturbed concern or doing can occur as the omission of something. When compared with this it becomes immediately apparent that in the latter sense, the expression "deficient mode" really designates something fundamentally different, which remains inconspicuous here only because Heidegger articulates it in its most innocuous form. For in comparison with instances of omission, all these instances of "disturbed" concern must properly count as instances of a concern that fails, is ineffectual, or miscarries.

As Heidegger himself emphasizes throughout, even in such instances concern is in principle always directed toward something definite, for example, toward driving in a nail with a hammer; only because, for example, this hammer turns out to be "damaged" is concern able in such instances not to succeed but rather—precisely by being directed toward this "something definite"—to fail. It remains entirely incomprehensible how Heidegger's way of speaking—that concern can sometimes occur as "disturbed"—could be maintained in any other sense than that such concern, for whatever reasons, can sometimes stray from its objective and hence remain unsuccessful with respect to this original objective.

But when compared with a doing or concern that succeeds, that which fails is a "deficient mode" of these in a fundamentally different sense than letting be is when compared with taking action. For regardless of whether doing or concern is now directed toward something in the first sense as a mode of taking action or as a "deficient" mode of letting be—as either of these modes it can still occur in the latter sense as a mode of successful action or as a "deficient" mode of unsuccessful action. In the omission of something, one can be just as successful or unsuccessful as in taking some kind of action.

Once this much has been made clear, one is in a position to explain further why it does not occur to Heidegger that this "disturbed" concern can really mean only failed or unsuccessful concern.

This is due entirely to the fact that Heidegger develops this "deficient" mode of concern solely on the basis of onesidedly selected examples. That is, he cites as "disturbed" concern exclusively those instances where that which "disturbs" is always discovered as "that which disturbs"—and indeed, it is discovered by just that circumspection which fundamentally guides all concern, even "disturbed" concern. In all three cases specified by Heidegger—in the case of equipment that is "damaged," "stands in the way," or is "missing"—beings are also *discovered as such*: they are recognized as something damaged, standing in the way, or missing, and hence are circumspectively recognized *as something which thus disturbs* (cf. pp. 73f).

From this it is apparent, first of all, that the "deficient" concern which Heidegger develops by means of these examples can in no way be regarded as "disturbed," as if circumspection there (under whose guidance concern always stands) were perhaps "disturbed." On the contrary, the circumspective knowing of that which disturbs is itself as such wholly undisturbed, so that in fact only those dealings that are guided by circumspection can count as "disturbed"; and this means that only doing that is guided by circumspective knowing can count as "disturbed." It is on account of that which disturbs, which itself is circumspectively known, that doing is capable of not reaching its objective; and thus, as a doing that is "disturbed" with respect to this objective, it remains quite authentically an unsuccessful doing.

But here it also becomes apparent just why this does not occur to Heidegger.

For if, instead of assuming, as Heidegger onesidedly does here, that the guiding circumspection were undisturbed, we assumed instead that it were itself disturbed in the sense that it did *not* discover "that which disturbs," the failure of this doing would then become even more conspicuous. Such an assumption within this theory is not simply permissible, but on the contrary virtually required—not only because Heidegger himself conceives this circumspection as an instance of concern and hence as something that can also sometimes occur in the "deficient" mode of a "disturbance," but rather also because Heidegger himself (as mentioned) posits this circumspection as something in which Dasein can sometimes "go wrong" as well (cf. p. 138).

Suppose, then, that circumspection could in fact take the form of "going wrong," for instance, if Dasein were not to discover that the hammer with which it wants to drive in a nail is damaged (for example, since its head is attached only very loosely to its handle). In this case Dasein would undoubtedly raise the hammer to strike, but instead of hitting the head of the nail it might possibly hit its own head or even another Dasein's head. Like the previous instance, this too would be an instance of "disturbed" concern in the sense of a doing that fails, but one whose failure (in contrast with the former) would no longer remain inconspicuous, because it would no longer be harmless.

On the contrary, this "disturbed" concern is indeed so conspicuously a failure that by comparison the failure in the former instance again threatens to get lost and so must again be expressly secured. If Dasein had discovered this damage instead of overlooking it, then rather than raising the hammer to strike, Dasein would, for instance, have fixed it or replaced it with an undamaged one—and then there might have been an instance of "undisturbed," successful concern. But as this Being-directed toward driving in a nail, it is and remains in principle a "disturbed" instance of concern that fails, precisely inasmuch as it is now concerned with the damaged hammer rather than with driving in the nail. It could certainly become conspicuous as a failure in this case too, if it were not a harmless case—for instance, if it were one in which a fragile piece of furniture that was supposed to be strengthened by driving in a nail were to collapse in the process.

If one keeps all this in view, then the following becomes clear: this revision of Heidegger's basic position does in fact lead to a result that is substantively and systematically significant, because it unites in itself the two basic ideas of the presence-at-hand and the readiness-to-hand of beings and thereby fundamentally preserves them both.

As already shown, Heidegger must ultimately recognize circumspection regarding ready-to-hand equipment as knowledge of present-at-hand things. This means that circumspection can no longer be regarded as something "pre-predica-tive," but must rather itself already count as a "determination" or "consideration" of "something as something" in the full sense of predication, and hence as knowledge of the present-at-hand which can be true or false. And this especially since Hei-degger himself admits that circumspection—as a primordial perception of beings—can sometimes occur in the mode of a "mistake," of a perceptual error, and hence can occur in principle as true or false perception.

This in no way means, however, that such primordial perception now has to count simply as pure knowledge of the present-at-hand, completely devoid of cir-cumspection regarding the ready-to-hand. Quite to the contrary, it becomes clear from the previous considerations that precisely insofar as this primordial perception itself is a true or false knowledge of the present-at-hand, not only can one maintain that it has a circumspective character regarding the ready-to-hand, but also that cir-cumspective character can really be sufficiently grounded only by this perception.

It has become clear that Heidegger considers concern to be something that can occur in the "deficient" mode of a "disturbed" concern, and hence fundamentally as "undisturbed" or "disturbed." It has also become clear that, on the other hand, he envisages the circumspection which guides concern as exclusively undisturbed. Since according to Heidegger it is itself supposed to be an instance of concern, even this circumspection must, as already noted, be considered as something that can occur in principle as either "disturbed" or "undisturbed." And as also noted above, there is a certain connection here: whether an instance of concern occurs as "disturbed" or "undisturbed" is apparently not independent of whether the circumspection that guides it occurs as "disturbed" or "undisturbed."

The real result here is that a "disturbed" or "undisturbed" instance of concern can really mean only a "successful" or "unsuccessful" instance of concern. An indica-tion of this is once again to be seen in the fact that for Heidegger, concern is really to be understood only as doing, and therefore the only way to understand "undis-turbed" or "disturbed" concern is as "successful" or "unsuccessful" action. But the fact that even circumspection can occur as "disturbed" or "undisturbed" would then have to mean that only a "successful" or "unsuccessful" circumspection can really be understood here, and this is the case especially because Heidegger attempts to con-ceive circumspection fundamentally as an instance of concern. Since only "going wrong," or a perceptual error (i.e., falsity in circumspection), can count as a "failure" of circumspection, it follows that an instance in which circumspection occurs as true perception rather than as "going wrong" (i.e., all truth in circumspection) would accordingly have to count as a "success."

But with this Heidegger's basic position would in fact be revised in a substantively and systematically significant way, and this revision can be developed and supported in detail.

First, it is finally clear that in fact knowing fundamentally resists every attempt to dissolve it into doing under the rubric of "concern." However appropriate it may be to view not only doing but also knowing as something that can occur as a success or a failure, they remain fundamentally distinct from one another as a success or failure *of doing*, on the one hand, and a success or failure *of knowledge*, on the other. This becomes quite clear from the fact that it is entirely possible to call a true cognition a successful cognition, while, on the other hand, it would be impossible in principle to talk about a successful action as a true action.

It becomes apparent from this that expressions like "success" or "successful" and hence their opposites like "unsuccessful" and "failure" possess their normal, non-metaphorical senses solely as characterizations of doing; a success or a failure is, in the normal sense of the word, always a success or failure *of doing*. Hence as characterizations of knowing, expressions like "success" or "failure" are only metaphors for something which we normally (without such expressions) characterize rightly as the "truth" or "falsity" of knowing.

And yet expressions like "success" or "failure" are metaphors for "truth" and "falsity" that are obviously possible and hence legitimate, since characterizations like the "success" or "failure" of knowing can make explicit something that is in fact contained implicitly in the "truth" or "falsity" of knowing.[1] What such expressions thus make explicit for the first time is nothing less than the exact sense in which primordial perception, understood as true or false knowledge—the theoretical as such—already itself has practical import and hence is ultimately circumspection. On the other hand, given truth or falsity as the success or failure of knowing, the converse manner of speaking, according to which we would call successful or unsuccessful doing something true or false, remains impossible and illegitimate because there exists (apparently in spite of this practical import of the theoretical itself) a fundamental difference between knowing and doing or theory and practice.

How is it to be explained, then, that in spite of this fundamental difference it is not first doing but rather knowing which always occurs as a success or a failure?

In the end the explanation for this lies in the fact that in both—not just in doing but rather already in knowing as well—something is intended and hence achieved or fallen short of, so that both are kinds of intentionality. For only where something is fundamentally intended does it make sense to ask whether the intention that occurs there is successful or unsuccessful, that is, whether it becomes a success or a failure.

If, for example, the wind blows a tile off the roof and it falls on someone's head on the street below, then it makes no sense at all to speak of the success or failure of the wind here, because the wind did not "throw" the tile—it did not "act on an intention"—as a subject or Dasein might. And with the insight that the truth and falsity of knowing are now to be conceived as the success or failure of knowing, the old insight—that not only doing but rather knowing as well always occur as specific instances of intentionality—is reinforced even further. In turn this ultimately leads to the fact that the common distinction between knowing as "noesis" and knowing as "noema" (which Heidegger critically opposes anyway—cf. pp. 155f., 216f.) needs to be revised in a certain respect.

This distinction is affected above all in the sense that truth or falsity applies to the noema as opposed to the noesis, that is, the "ideal" content of knowledge as opposed to the "real" *act* of knowledge (cf. ibid.). Now, if it is correct that truth emerges as the success of knowing and falsity emerges as its failure, then the two can be meaningfully ascribed only to something that permits a corresponding intention to be meaningfully ascribed to it as well. But the noema as opposed to the noesis can never be understood as an intention, since the noema as such intends nothing at all, that is, it is in no way intentional; rather, in principle only the noesis does this. As the act of knowledge, only the noesis can count meaningfully as such an intention, and hence as successful or unsuccessful—as true or false—in regard to that intention.

But this is so, of course, not simply in the sense that the noesis as opposed to the noema would now be true or false; rather, this noema (as something into which the noesis always forms itself) is also the very *way* in which the noesis forms itself into something true (and thus is successful) or into something false (and thus is unsuccessful). Be it ever so difficult to work out this idea of the noesis forming *itself* into the noema (and this ultimately means thinking noesis and noema as a difference within an *identity*), it is important to see the positive sense of this very difficulty. For it makes it clear that only this idea can protect a working out of the relationship between noesis and noema from an untenable Platonism of the noema over the noesis.

The fact that one can thus speak meaningfully of both success or failure in doing, and of truth or falsity as success or failure in knowing, only where there is a corresponding intention, simply cannot mean that truth and falsity or success and failure can meaningfully be spoken of only where *both* of these are intended. The fundamental reason for this is that it would make no sense for a subject or Dasein *to intend to fail* in doing in the same way that it intends to succeed in doing, nor would it make sense for it *to intend falsity* as a *failure* in knowing in the same way that it intends a *success* (i.e., *truth*) in knowing. As the origin and principle of the intention of something, a subject or Dasein instead primordially and fundamentally intends only success, never failure.

Therefore, if such a failure nonetheless occurs, in principle it must have the character of something that does no more than interfere with (*unterläuft*) a subject or Dasein. This applies not only to doing but also to knowing: just as doing can be understood in principle only as the intention of a subject or Dasein to succeed, knowing too can be understood only as the intention to succeed—and in principle this means that it can be understood only as the intention of a subject or Dasein toward truth. Likewise, if falsity occurs as a failure, it too can count in principle only as something that simply interferes with a subject or Dasein, and thus as unintended falsity it is nothing more than an error.

From this it is apparent that error (as unintended falsity) constitutes the exact opposite of lying (as intended falsity), an opposition which here coincides with that between knowing and doing. For mere error is still an instance of knowing, whereas a lie is an instance of doing. Thus there is a fundamental dichotomy between error and lie, which one often thinks one has to neglect for the sake of phenomena like "ideology" (Marx) or "repression" (Freud).[2] In my judgment, however, this is certainly unjustified, since on closer inspection it may turn out that the very occurrence of such phenomena depends upon the strict dichotomy between error and lie.

The fact that this remains unclear is also related to the fact that talk of an "interest in untruth"[3] (and this does mean talk of an "interest in falsity") is not univocal. For something like "untruth" or "falsity" can in principle never occur in the abstract, but instead can only occur concretely as either intended or unintended falsity—and thus as either lie or error. If one now proceeds accordingly, it becomes apparent immediately that this way of speaking cannot mean both of these, as it purports to, because fundamentally the only possibility here is to have an "interest in lying," while on the contrary something like an "interest in error" (and here what is meant is naturally *one's own* error, just as with lying) remains utterly impossible for the reasons given above.[4]

But from the fact that not only doing but also knowing can emerge in principle only as an intention to succeed, and hence that the truth of knowing as well must always count as the success of the intention toward the truth of this very knowing, it is also clear that the practical import of theory is already present right here. And the presence of this practical import makes it evident that knowing does not emerge simply as true or false "theoretical" knowledge of present-at-hand things, but instead emerges at the same time as "practical" circumspection regarding ready-to-hand equipment as well. For from the fact that it is not only appropriate but virtually required here to call the truth or falsity of knowing (and not just doing) "success" or "failure," it becomes clear that there may be connections both between this truth and success in doing and between this falsity and failure in doing.

In fact it is also incomprehensible how an action could ever succeed except on the assumption that the knowledge whose content is relevant to this action has itself already succeeded and hence is true knowledge. Accordingly it remains equally incomprehensible how an action could ever fail except on the assumption that the knowledge whose content is relevant to this action has itself already failed and hence is false knowledge.

One might raise the following objection against this: even if all knowledge whose content is relevant to a certain action is true knowledge, such an action can always still fail because, for example, the physical strength of a subject or Dasein does not suffice for it to succeed. But with this objection one would be oversimplifying things. One need only assume that one "surely knew" one's physical strength to be insufficient for the action, and it will immediately become unintelligible how a subject or Dasein could ever have undertaken this action at all.

On the other hand, this means that a subject's or Dasein's having undertaken something like an action is intelligible in general only to the extent that it "takes as its point of departure" the sufficiency of its physical strength for the action. Of course it can err in this, but just on that account this is to be conceived as an instance in which action fails solely on the basis of a knowledge that has already failed (i.e., on the basis of error). And it must be granted that all similar objections can be refuted in the same way.

If one accepts this, it becomes clear for the first time that in just this respect Heidegger's discussion of "disturbed" concern must remain unintelligible. On the one hand (as already shown), "disturbed" concern can be understood only as a doing that fails; and on the other hand (as also already shown), Heidegger conceives of the circumspection which guides concern as undisturbed and hence as true knowledge.

But if, for example, the discovery of damage to a hammer is true knowledge, then it makes no sense at all to speak of a corresponding action (for example of driving in a nail with the hammer) as an action that fails.[5] Indeed, this is so not simply because it remains unintelligible in principle how a subject or Dasein who has discovered damage to a hammer might also attempt to drive in a nail with this hammer.[6] On the contrary, this could become intelligible *only* to the extent that this subject or Dasein actually errs about this damage, and that means taking the hammer precisely as undamaged and grasping it as a tool that has been taken to be suitable.

This means that in understanding "disturbed" concern as a doing that fails while also understanding undisturbed circumspection as true knowledge, Heidegger brings things together that do not belong together at all: as a doing that fails, an attempt to drive in a nail with a hammer is intelligible only insofar as the circumspection which guides this attempt has *not* recognized the damage to the hammer; on the other hand, only a doing that is fundamentally different from this doing that fails—for example, the attempt to fix the hammer or to exchange it for an undamaged one—only this kind of doing is intelligible in the context that was Heidegger's point of departure, namely, that in which the damage to the hammer has been recognized.

Thus a doing that fails is intelligible only where the knowing that guides it fails, and successful doing is in turn intelligible only where the knowing that guides it succeeds. From this the fact that knowing, as something purely theoretical, has practical import becomes apparent in the following: a subject or Dasein intends knowing (i.e., truth as success in knowing) precisely as the *means* without which success in doing (which is what it really intends) simply could not take place. But with this there results yet another revision in Heidegger's position, one which is as substantively and systematically interesting as the previous one.

NOTES

1. As a corresponding and equally legitimate metaphor, one must be able to characterize even knowing itself, which always emerges in the form of a judgment, as doing: as an *act* of knowledge or judgment. Cf. also pp. 41ff. below.
2. Cf., e.g., Ernst Tugendhat, *Der Wahrheitsbegriff bei Husserl und Heidegger*, 2nd ed. (Berlin: De Gruyter, 1970), p. 325.
3. Ibid., pp. 320f., 322ff.
4. Naturally this insight presupposes further that one also bear in mind the difference in principle between an "interest in error" (which is impossible) and an "interest in forgetting" (which is indeed possible), a difference which is essential for a more exact analysis of anything like "ideology" or "repression."
5. Unless some other knowledge that were relevant here were erroneous-false knowledge—which must nonetheless be left out of consideration here because it would amount to a *petitio principii.*
6. The normal sense of "driving in" is of course to be maintained here and is not to be altered so as to take on the sense of "cautiously driving in."

5.

The Real Primacy of Doing over Knowing

The character of knowing as a *means*, which has just now become clear, confirms, on the one hand, that knowing as theory has practical import, that is, that as true or false knowledge of the present-at-hand it is itself circumspection regarding the ready-to-hand. But, on the other hand, this very character of knowing as a means immediately presents a new problem. For it is just this character of being a *means* that Heidegger sees in beings in Dasein's environment and sets forth as the equipmental or ready-to-hand character of these beings.

Is then knowing itself perhaps to be conceived exclusively as something like ready-to-hand equipment, since as circumspection it too has this character—is it then to be conceived as a mere being in Dasein's environment?

There is no doubt that this question must be answered negatively—indeed Heidegger himself does so. But there is also no doubt that the character of being a means, which in any case knowing has, then immediately gives rise to the converse question: Is it in fact this kind of mere being in Dasein's environment, a being that has the character of being a means, that leads Heidegger to conceive knowing as ready-to-hand equipment?

That nonetheless this question too can only be answered negatively is by no means obvious to Heidegger. On the contrary, the extremely spirited and justifiably renowned analyses in ¶¶15–18, where Heidegger develops the structure of beings in Dasein's environment as the structure of "involvement" of ready-to-hand equipment, are among the most convincing ones in Heidegger's *Being and Time*. These beings are always recognized primordially by circumspective knowing in contexts of an "involvement," that is, in means-ends relations in which such ends themselves are in turn only means for further ends, relations that always terminate in Dasein itself. For as the being for whom "in its very Being, that Being is an *issue* for it" (p. 12), only Dasein exists as an ultimate "for-the-sake-of" (pp. 84ff.), as a final end in relation to which all other ends can ultimately be mere means, while Dasein itself can never be a mere means.[1]

35

In the course of his analyses Heidegger's continual ascription of the character of being a means to mere beings themselves as such, to equipment as ready-to-hand, is all the more convincing at first since he develops it simply as a theory that accords with everyone's most everyday convictions. It is beings themselves as such which are, for example, means for writing and hence writing implements, or are, for example, means for driving and hence vehicles.[2] Heidegger expresses this conviction so decisively that in his theory he even says that the equipmental character of these ready-to-hand beings (and hence their character as means) constitutes the "being-in-itself" of these beings, that it is the way in which these beings are " in-themselves."[3]

But even if such a philosophical theory makes that everyday conviction nearly self-evident, it cannot be maintained. One need only assume it to be impossible in principle (for whatever reason) for Dasein to get to a being like a writing implement or a vehicle, and one suddenly sees that the character of being a means which supposedly applies to these beings "in-themselves" applies in truth to something fundamentally different from them. This assumption suffices to alienate the beings quite familiar to us as means, to such an extent that their character as means virtually falls away from them as a mere appearance and at once comes forward in something fundamentally different than these beings. It is not a writing implement itself, not this being as such, but rather the *grasping* of a writing implement, the *guiding* of a writing implement, and the like which are means for writing; and it is not a vehicle itself, not this being as such, but rather the *boarding* of a vehicle, the *steering* of a vehicle, and the like which are means for driving.

But this is to say that upon closer examination, such a means for an action is in each instance itself an action and nothing like the mere being itself that one deals with in an action. It simply cannot be ignored that a counterexample could always be found here: no matter how far one might trace an action back to the *means* for this action, in each case one finds it necessary once again, in keeping with this consideration, to posit as the *means* for an action what amounts to the *grasping of* a being rather than this being itself. And if one ignores the possibility of such ways of *approaching* beings and *dealing with* them, as happens in Heidegger's assumption above, then along with these ways of acting (which are the real means for doing) the character of being a means (which only *seems* to apply to beings themselves) also disappears.

From this it is also apparent that our everyday conviction—that the character of being a means applies to beings themselves—ultimately derives from the fact that we transfer this character of being a means, which is really the character of being an activity and hence is a property of us as Dasein, from ourselves to beings other than Dasein. But it is still more astonishing that, even when conceiving it philosophically, Heidegger himself appropriates this conviction without qualification. For this conviction is indicative of a tendency in Dasein's self-understanding, one that Heidegger more appropriately than anyone before him characterizes as the "fallenness" of Dasein.

But he sees this false self-understanding quite onesidedly, in that he focuses entirely on Dasein's tendency to understand itself exclusively in terms of beings in its environment, which it does by ascribing to itself characteristics that are distinctive only of beings other than Dasein, thereby misunderstanding its own distinctiveness (cf., e.g., pp. 15, 21, 175ff.). But such fallenness of Dasein is likewise present when, conversely, it attributes to beings in its environment characteristics that are peculiar to Dasein alone, because this too amounts to a self-misunderstanding—a misunderstanding of its own distinctiveness.

This is exactly what happens when Heidegger, in the spirit of our everyday conviction, attributes this character of being a means to beings "in themselves," to ready-to-hand equipment in Dasein's environment—a fallenness and self-misunderstanding of Dasein that borders closely on an occult conception of the environment.

This becomes clear particularly in ¶16, where Heidegger contrasts "disturbed" concern with undisturbed concern. He conceives means-end relations there quite explicitly as the "peculiar and self-evident 'in itself'" of beings as such, as "references" within ready-to-hand equipment itself (p. 74), as if these beings as such could "refer" to other beings and hence do something. Then he traces undisturbed concern back to a "ready-to-hand as 'holding itself in,'" as if this very being controls itself in order not to disturb concern; and he then correspondingly traces disturbed concern back to a "break" in the "referential context" of equipment, as if these beings themselves let themselves go and thereby disturbed concern (pp. 75, 80).

But in fact these beings themselves are what they are, and the activity of Dasein cannot but succeed if these beings are themselves recognized by Dasein. It borders on mystification to ascribe to beings themselves activities like "holding themselves in" or "disturbing. " A "disturbed" or "undisturbed" concern can meaningfully be traced back only to Dasein itself. Not only does Dasein itself always procure something like a means for its activity; in all this activity Dasein is "undisturbed" (and that means genuinely successful) just as long as it is likewise successful with the means which it must in each instance begin by creating, that is, as long as it is likewise successful in knowing.

Hence if knowing itself were set forth as the necessary means for activity, it would by no means follow that this knowing would thus become reified into ready-to-hand equipment in Dasein's environment and consequently into a mere being. On the contrary, this insight even leads to the overcoming (*bereinigen*) of a reification (and hence of a fallenness that worked its way into even Heidegger's thinking), because at the same time it gives rise to the further insight that a mere being can fundamentally never be anything like a means for doing. In contrast to "ready-to-hand equipment," which in *Being and Time* as well as in everydayness gets conceived as means for activity, the actual means for activity is in reality always, as has been shown, itself an activity and hence no mere being in Dasein's environment—it is neither something ready-to-hand nor something present-at-hand, but rather just Dasein itself.

Of course this insight—gained first of all only as a correction of that everyday conviction shared by Heidegger—must, in order to remain correct, be qualified. This qualification is important because it also offers the possibility of clarifying, if only initially, the special relationship—first of all the distinction and then the connection—between knowing and doing.

For as certainly as it is correct that, as opposed to ready-to-hand equipment as mere beings, the actual means for activity is in each instance itself an activity, it is just as certain that one must acknowledge an important exception to this last statement: There is at least one means for activity which, on the one hand, is not a mere being but which, on the other hand, is itself also not an activity, and this means is knowing. As opposed to mere beings in Dasein's environment, neither knowing nor doing is either ready-to-hand or present-at-hand; rather, they are ways in which a human being in each case *is*, that is, they are Dasein itself. Indeed, in contrast to Dasein's activity and all those means for activity that themselves turn out to be actions, Dasein's knowing is evidently the sole means for activity that itself does not turn out to be activity.

The negative aspect of this characterization of knowing in relation to Dasein's activity can be turned into a positive one if we look back once more at our insight into the essence of activity (cf. above pp. 19ff.).

In connection with his example of "making" something out of something, for example, making a plate out of wood, Heidegger conceives doing quite appropriately as essentially an intention to change beings. In terms of his own explications this means, in the first place, that it would remain unintelligible in principle to speak here of a Dasein aiming its activity at something that is already actual (wood), unless it were mistaken about this. Accordingly its activity is fundamentally directed instead toward something that is not yet actual but is merely possible (plate), precisely in order to actualize it; and this doing is directed toward something already actual only in order to change it (wood).

But however illuminating this last point may be at first glance, on closer examination it proves to be problematic. If it is correct that doing can fundamentally never be directed toward "something already actual," then the qualification "only in order to change it" is no longer of any use whatsoever; and then the whole assertion that doing is directed "toward something already actual only in order to change it" must instead be partly false. But this then leads to a fundamental problem.

That in fact doing must always be somehow directed toward beings like wood, and hence toward something already actual, is not only shown by this particular example of making a plate out of wood, but can also be shown to be true in general. From the very beginning, something like doing is intelligible only to the extent that it occurs in the kind of being that, like human Dasein, is, on the one hand, finitely limited and is, on the other hand, still in need of all those things that are related to it in spite of this limitedness. Dasein must from the very beginning direct its doing, as the attempt to satisfy this neediness, beyond itself and its limitedness, and this means toward beings other than itself. But note: toward beings and hence toward something already actual.

And therein lies the fundamental problem: Can something like doing (which indeed essentially directs itself toward the actualization of something, and hence toward something not yet actual) also direct itself toward something already actual?

If one considers this question precisely, then one must answer it strictly in the negative: it is utterly impossible that anything like doing could direct itself toward something already actual in the same way that it directs itself toward something not yet actual. Insofar as doing as such directs itself toward what is not yet actual, doing must instead direct itself in each case *beyond* what is already actual. Here one will do well to clarify this fundamental impossibility (or rather, necessity) by means of a very simple example, for which once again the production of a plate out of wood may serve.

As regards the wood, then, an activity (as an intention to actualize something) that directs itself first of all toward actualizing the wood itself and as such, remains utterly unintelligible. An activity becomes intelligible in principle only to the extent that it directs itself toward something that, given the presence of the wood, is not yet actual but rather lies beyond the actuality of the wood—for example, toward removing a piece (be it ever so small) of this wood with a first cut of the knife and thereby making a first step beyond this actual wood toward the not-yet-actual plate.

Incidentally, this consideration confirms once again that a means for an activity like making a plate is in each case itself an activity and never simply a mere being like the wood: each such individual cut is a means for this making, and all of these together finally yield a plate. The same applies to everything that can happen to this wood prior to the first cut, to laying out and even to taking hold of the wood. As activity, all of this is intelligible in principle only insofar as it directs itself in each case toward something that in relation to the wood is not yet actual—in this last case toward giving the wood a new spatial location, one that is more favorable for cutting.

But then the fundamental problem mentioned above becomes almost paradoxical.

For there is no doubt whatsoever that in all of these cases, activity, even though in each case it fundamentally directs itself beyond what is actual toward something not yet actual, is indeed also directed in each case toward what *is* actual. From the example under consideration, it is clear that the making of a plate is directed as much toward the wood as such in each individual phase as it is directed beyond the wood per se and toward the plate. For however far one may trace all of these individual phases back to the primordial appropriation of the wood, each one of these is always still an activity, which as such itself is also always directed once again beyond what is actual toward something that is not yet actual; and nonetheless each also directs itself toward what is already actual.

How, then, is activity directed from start to finish toward what in each case is itself actual?

Not in virtue of itself, this much is clear; not in virtue of that which as doing it essentially is, namely, an intention to actualize something not yet actual, for as such it is *essentially* directed precisely toward what is not yet actual.

But in virtue of what else, then?

The answer can only be: *solely* in virtue of knowing. The most primordial way in which human Dasein as a finitely limited being is capable of coming upon other beings at all, and what must precede the most primordial taking possession of such beings (i.e., doing), is knowing. In virtue of this knowing, doing (which as such is always directed beyond what is actual toward what is not yet actual) directs itself in each of its individual phases first of all toward what is actual. If Dasein is capable of satisfying its neediness, which motivates it as a finitely limited being, only through its acting on other beings, it is never capable of acquiring such beings primordially through this activity itself and as such. For these beings, as already actual, must instead be acquired *for* this activity (as the intention toward what is not yet actual).

But as such a precondition for activity, beings in fact cannot be acquired through activity per se but instead only through the fact that Dasein separates out for itself, so to speak, precisely on the basis of its intention to act (and this means toward making this very activity itself possible), a particular intention to know: Dasein is capable of primordially acquiring something like a being that is already actual (and hence capable of fulfilling the precondition for doing as the actualization of what is not yet actual), first of all as an object for this very knowing. This likewise applies for each individual phase of doing that may be able to be distinguished as a distinct action within a broader context of action.

If one bears all this in mind, then it becomes apparent that knowing and doing in fact stand in a very special relationship to one another, because in spite of their fundamental distinctness they still form such a strict unity with one another that apparently neither can occur without the other—neither doing without knowing, nor knowing without doing.

The previously developed insight simply cannot be recast merely by saying that knowing is just the kind of intention that directs itself toward what is already actual, and that doing is just the kind of intention that directs itself toward what is not yet actual (cf. above pp. 19ff.). For in this recasting the decisive point would be lost, namely, that even doing is itself directed toward what is already actual—even if only by means of knowing. It would be a decisive abbreviation of that insight simply to say that knowing is that which directs itself toward what is already actual, when in fact according to this insight that which truly directs itself toward what is already actual is really doing—except that on the whole doing directs itself, as it were, only in virtue of knowing.

Accordingly it is not really knowing which directs itself toward what is already actual; rather, knowing is instead nothing but the way in which doing directs itself toward what is already actual, and yet precisely as doing it does not remain static but instead directs itself beyond knowing (though with its help) toward what is not yet actual. Hence even though they each intend something different, knowing and doing by no means occur as two diverse intentions alongside one another, but instead ultimately occur only as one single intention (complex though it may be) which from the start is to be addressed as doing.

And yet this intention must from the start and as such branch out beyond itself and must, so to speak, consign itself first of all to knowing, because in general it is capable of being activity only by means of knowing. Therefore, that something like an intention to know can emerge at all in Dasein has its ground solely in the fact that it emerges only as a necessary component of an entire intention, which by no means terminates in knowing (which it first intends) but rather terminates, with the help of this knowing, in doing (toward which Dasein in each case really aims).

Only in this way can what was previously only linguistically intelligible become substantively explicable, namely, that knowing is to be characterized (if only metaphorically) as a doing—as an *act* of knowing or judgment (cf. above p. 34, n. 1); the legitimacy of this metaphor is clear from the fact that the truth or falsity of knowing is likewise to be characterized as the success or failure of such doing. Now, this linguistic finding has its substantive explanation in the fact that, as fundamentally distinct as knowing and doing are and remain, to conceive Dasein's knowing *fundamentally* is actually to conceive its doing as well—precisely because it intends something like knowing in general only on the basis of the intention to act, and this in turn only because first of all it needs to succeed in knowing in order to succeed in doing (which is all it ultimately strives for).

For it is solely for the sake of *true* knowing, toward the *object* of knowing, that Dasein in each case primordially acquires beings that are already actual; and it is solely on the basis of this that Dasein, in virtue of successful activity on the basis of what is already actual, is then capable of first of all actualizing something in it that is not yet actual.

Only with this do we reach the point where it becomes fully evident how special (but also how complicated) the relationship between knowing and doing really is. If, first of all, it was a matter of establishing, against Heidegger, that knowing and theory in every case possess a primacy over doing and practice, just now it was instead a matter of showing that in spite of this primacy over practice, theory as such itself has practical import and is thus (as knowledge of the present-at-hand) itself circumspection regarding the ready-to-hand (precisely in Heidegger's sense).

Nonetheless the insight into the way in which theory is in fact circumspection ultimately amounts to nothing less than the acknowledgment of a primacy of practice over theory, and hence on the whole to something obviously paradoxical. For with the fact that in every case knowing emerges as a necessary means for doing, the fact that in every case knowing also possesses this primacy over doing remains established; given the fact that, nonetheless, this very knowing emerges as such a means for doing not *as* doing but rather *in virtue of* doing, one cannot fail to see that there also exists a converse primacy of doing over knowing.

The final implication of this apparent paradox, which occurs as the end result of this substantive and systematic revision of the position in *Being and Time*, is quite clear: if Heidegger had carried out this revision himself, he would have had to return to a conception of the "subjectivity of the subject" like the one attempted by Kant and by the German Idealists in connection with him.

This is also particularly clear given the fact that the special relationship that exists between knowing and "intuition" is repeated once again, in a comparable way, in the relationship between doing and knowing as it was first developed above. Just as knowing is the means for doing, "intuition" is the means for knowing. And just as doing consists in each case in going beyond what is actual and known (or rather, what is actual and objectified) and proceeding toward the actualization of something that is not yet actual, knowing consists in each case in going beyond such "intuition" (as a private and subjective "internal world") and proceeding toward the objectification of the intersubjective and objective "external world," as the actuality to be known.

The comparability of these two relationships becomes all the more obvious if one also notes the extent to which doing and knowing are in every case mediated and yet also immediate.

For although doing is mediated by knowing what is actual, it still remains immediate in relation to that toward which it directs itself as doing, namely, to what is not yet actual, toward whose actualization it aims; and indeed this is so because, by itself, knowing is not yet doing. Surely one must acknowledge that it is only through the mediation of this knowing that doing is at all capable of being such an immediacy.

A corresponding point also holds for knowing. For although it is likewise mediated by "intuition," it still remains immediate in relation to that toward which it directs itself, namely, that which is already actual, which it seeks to know, that is, to objectify; the reason for this "intuition" itself is neither knowledge nor object. Here, too, one will even have to say that only through the mediation of "intuition" is anything like the immediate knowledge (or rather, immediate objectivity) of something capable of emerging at all.

With this there would be a good chance of unifying the theories of the knowing and doing of subjectivity in a complete, "transcendental" theory of subjectivity, because, in both, something like subjectivity would ultimately manifest itself as the repeated giving of form to a material, in which what is formed and what is thereby obtained would simply exchange roles, in an ever further giving of form. So, for example, what is obtained through knowing (something actual understood as an object) would be what is formed in doing, but not at all what is obtained through doing: it would therefore be only what is being acted upon, and not at all what is achieved. The correctly understood primacy of practice over theory, just as that of theory over practice, would thus involve the most primordial "acceptance" of "intuition" in knowing, because in knowing, intuition would be what is thus formed, even if it would not be what is thus obtained.

However, the apparent paradox in there being a primacy of knowing over doing, as well as one of doing over knowing, could be eliminated only through considering that this former primacy has by no means the same sense as the latter one. The distinct senses in which on the one hand knowing possesses a primacy over doing and on the other hand doing possesses a primacy over knowing, can indeed be determined only if one transfers the distinction between knowing in the sense of noema and knowing in the sense of noesis to doing, and in exactly the same way distinguishes, here too, between doing in the sense of poiema and doing in the sense of poiesis.

In the case of knowing, as already noted, what is meant by "noema" as opposed to "noesis" is the *content* of knowledge as opposed to the *act* of knowledge, and hence that through which, for example, a cognition like "this hammer is damaged" differs from another cognition like "this is wood"; whereas, apart from this, one cognition does *not* differ from another such cognition simply in virtue of its *act* of knowledge, as noesis. As an act of knowledge or noesis, knowing is rather always the same, namely, the intention of a subject or Dasein to acquire for itself some being or actual thing as an object by shaping it into a definite noema, and hence to succeed in truly knowing such an object.

But something corresponding exactly to this would emerge by distinguishing the poiema from the poiesis, the content of doing from the act of doing, namely, that through which, for example, an action like "driving in a nail with a hammer" differs from another action like "making a plate out of wood"; whereas, apart from this, one action does *not* differ from another action simply in virtue of its act of doing, as poiesis. Rather, as an act of doing, or poiesis, doing is always the same, namely, the intention of a subject or Dasein to actualize something not yet actual from out of what is already actual by shaping it into a definite poiema, and hence to succeed in acting on something thus actualized.

With the help of this distinction, one could in fact specify the distinct senses of primacy—in which knowing has a primacy over doing and doing has a primacy over knowing.

The sense in which there is a primacy of knowing over doing (namely, that success in doing is possible only on the basis of a success in the knowing relevant to that doing) would accordingly consist precisely in the fact that doing *as poiema* would be dependent on knowing *as noema*. A Dasein would be successful in virtue of the definite poiema into which the poiesis itself of that Dasein takes shape, only if that Dasein were also successful in virtue of the definite noema into which its relevant noesis itself takes shape.

On the other hand, the sense in which there is a primacy of doing over knowing (namely, that in general something like an intention to know occurs only insofar as something like an intention to act occurs) would accordingly consist in the fact that knowing *as noesis* would be dependent on doing *as poiesis*. Regardless of whether a noesis is formed into this noema or that one, and regardless of whether Dasein is successful or not with the noema into which its noesis is formed—this noesis itself, which Dasein must in each case allow to come to pass, can come to pass at all only because in an engagement with this noesis itself Dasein is already directed further toward poiesis, and can be so directed in general only in virtue of such noesis.

But not only the distinction between knowing and doing, but also, in the case of knowing, the distinction between noema and noesis, and in the case of doing, the distinction between poiema and poiesis—all of these distinctions would have to be thought of as difference within an identity, namely, as the most highly differentiated way in which a Dasein forms itself: as the structure of the "subjectivity of the subject."

NOTES

1. Cf. in this regard Martin Heidegger, *Logik: Die Frage nach der Wahrheit, Gesamtausgabe*, Vol. 21 (Frankfurt: Klostermann, 1976), p. 220, where Heidegger himself makes it known that in his characterization of Dasein in *Being and Time* as the ultimate "for-the-sake-of" he is taking his bearings from the characterization of the human being as "end in itself" and hence from Kant.
2. [*Translators' note*. The words translated "writing implements" and "vehicles" (*Schreibzeug* and *Fahrzeug*) both contain the root *Zeug*, which is the term translated by Macquarrie and Robinson in *Being and Time* as "equipment."]
3. Cf., e.g., pp. 69, 71, 74ff., 106.

6.

Practicism and Utopian Theoreticism

The revision of *Being and Time* just worked out, which results from the substantive and systematic difficulties of that work, has led to the insight that knowing and doing are to be thought together as the different ways in which a subject or Dasein forms itself. This revision could then renew the discussion of a theme that was central to Kant and the German Idealists, but which broke off after them. Indeed, quite in keeping with the spirit of these philosophers, it might well lead beyond that which limited them.

For the result of this revision is that in its aforementioned relationship with doing, knowing can be made intelligible only as a subject's intention *to succeed*, and hence the truth of knowing can be made intelligible only as the *success* of this subject's intention. But this insight amounts to a practicism of knowing and truth, which Kant and the German Idealists had only barely anticipated, and which Heidegger's practicistic theory of "circumspection" regarding "ready-to-hand equipment" in the "environment" simply leaves out of consideration.

This is especially apparent from the fact that this sense of knowing as an intention to succeed, and of truth as the success of a subject, applies in particular to the most elementary and primordial cases of knowing, namely to cases of perception, in which Dasein hears or sees, for example, other beings as its environment. And yet this means that the opposition between true perception and its objects, in which Dasein always primordially acquires other beings as actual, comes to be at all only to the extent that Dasein itself as a subject always first reaches the truth of knowing and with just this also reaches beings as actual. With the help of such a success, it always intends both of these solely in order to attain something entirely different, namely, success in doing. As actual things in the environment, beings are always perceived by Dasein from the start with an eye toward what can be done with them. As present-at-hand they are always acquired from the start as ready-to-hand; accordingly true knowledge, through which Dasein in each case acquires such beings, is from the start itself circumspection.

But after *Being and Time* Heidegger departs more and more decisively from this very practicism, which can be shown to be a logical consequence of *Being and Time* itself and which brings this work in line with the great works from Kant to Hegel and Schelling. The substantive and systematic difficulties in *Being and Time*, whose revision results in this practicism, were probably seen very early by Heidegger himself, but because of what it results in, Heidegger himself no longer works out this revision explicitly. For just this reason, instead of working out *Being and Time* further, Heidegger completes the "turning." This means that he lets go of *Being and Time*, with its substantive and systematic difficulties, and instead takes up and attempts to substantiate fundamentally what he would have to abandon in working out the revision of *Being and Time*: the conception of knowing as the mere "perception" of beings and of truth as the "unconcealedness" of these beings themselves, an unconcealedness which, in such knowing, Dasein always merely perceives along with the beings thus perceived.

As has been shown, already in *Being and Time* such θεωρία as "theoretical" knowing of the present-at-hand is not only not derivable from "practical" circumspection regarding the ready-to-hand, in the end it is not even distinguishable from it. Rather, what is "theoretical" is itself and as such what is "practical," and vice versa. But inasmuch as it coincides in this way with circumspection regarding the ready-to-hand, knowledge of the present-at-hand loses just the character of being purely theoretical which according to *Being and Time* it was supposed to possess. Even less could Heidegger turn a blind eye to this insight, given that it first enables us to see that the most distinctive case of this "theoretical" knowledge of the present-at-hand, namely, natural science, must also count as the distinctive case of "practical" circumspection regarding the ready-to-hand. As the comprehensive truth about beings, natural science is accordingly also a comprehensive success on Dasein's part with regard to viewing these beings; as the presupposition for the further comprehensive success with beings which Dasein attains in technology, this success in natural science makes its practical character distinctly known.

But in virtue of this coinciding with "practical" circumspection regarding the ready-to-hand, "theoretical" knowing of the present-at-hand would then lose just the character of pure receptivity (as a mere "perception" of beings in the sense of Aristotelian θεωρία) which, according to *Being and Time*, it was supposed to possess. In the most elementary and primordial cases of knowing, namely, in the everyday perception of beings in the environment, the whole spontaneity of Dasein is revealed in a knowing which is both "theoretical" and "practical"; and in this, Dasein is directed toward success in such knowing in general only in order, by means of it, to be directed toward success in doing. And yet this means that precisely the "subjectivity of the subject"—which in the end manifests its spontaneity in the complete unre-strainedness and intemperance of technology, to the point of a destruction of the world and a self-destruction—this very "subjectivity" of Dasein is at work from the beginning, in the origin of anything like the perception of something.

In connection with this insight, the conception of knowing as a merely recep-tive "perceiving" of beings and of truth as the "unconcealedness" of beings them-selves in this perception could no longer be maintained. Instead Heidegger would have been forced by this insight to give up once and for all such a receptive concep-tion of knowing and truth, which was taken over from antiquity and which has been outmoded at least since Kant. In its place he would have had to develop further a Kantian conception of knowing as spontaneous judging and of its truth as the suc-cess of knowledge or judgment, and hence to hold to the meaning of truth as the truth of knowledge or judgment. This is so especially since the receptive conception of the "perceiving" of something "unconcealed" is, when examined in itself, hardly convincing.

For whatever might be meant by a knowing "which perceives," understood as the "discovering" or "revealing" of beings, and by truth as the corresponding "dis-coveredness" or "unconcealedness" of beings (cf. pp. 212ff.), any conception of this kind necessarily fails purely in virtue of the fact that in principle it is unintelligible to say of a being, for example, a hammer or even some wood, that it is true.[1] And this applies as well to all interpretations that still attempt to make sense of this truth as the "truth of the matter" or the "truth of things."[2]

It may be that what these expressions mean is quite intelligible; nonetheless it remains entirely unintelligible what such expressions of "truth" could possibly con-tribute to our understanding.

For from the fact that it does make sense to speak, for example, of "true gold," it follows only that in this regard language is sufficiently metaphorical that it would be methodologically responsible to burden it with more of these unnecessary metaphors. On the other hand, in just this regard language is also sufficiently uni-vocal, because on the contrary a more careful consideration makes it clear that some-thing fundamentally different is meant by "true" gold and the like than what is meant by true knowledge[3]; and once given this sense of true knowledge, nothing other than such knowledge can fundamentally be true.

In spite of that insight into the full spontaneity and hence into the "subjec-tivity" of Dasein, not only does Heidegger not give up this conception of its recep-tivity in knowing and truth, but instead, right after achieving that insight, he vali-dates it fundamentally for the first time.

That in fact Heidegger himself was unable to turn a blind eye toward this

insight is clear from the fact that circumspective dealings with ready-to-hand equipment in the environment, which in *Being and Time* he valued in an entirely positive
way as Dasein's most primordial relationship to beings, are shortly thereafter evaluated by him in a much more negative way and then no longer discussed at all. In any
event, already in 1928 in the essay "On the Essence of Truth," where in a footnote
he does still mention these circumspective dealings with equipment, Heidegger suddenly no longer admits that in *Being and Time* he saw in them the origin of Dasein's
relationship to beings: he now suddenly plays down the "analysis of the environment" by claiming that in *Being and Time* it has only "subordinate significance," a
claim which can in no way be brought into accord with the text of that work. He
now claims just as unconvincingly that in the "ontological structure of beings
within-the-world . . . as equipment," which he laid out in this analysis, what can be
seen is by no means Dasein's primordial relationship to beings but rather something
that merely has "the advantage" of "leading up" to the analysis of this relationship
and "preparing" for its problematization (cf. "Vom Wesen des Grundes," *Wegmarken*,
2nd ed., p. 153n. [*The Essence of Reasons*, p. 81n.]). Apparently he now seeks emphatically to locate the origin of this relationship somewhere else.[4]

This is even more apparent when one considers the following. To precisely the
same extent that he now evaluates more negatively the circumspective dealings with
the ready-to-hand which he previously valued positively, Heidegger now begins as
well to value more positively the mere knowledge of the merely present-at-hand
which in *Being and Time* he had evaluated negatively, in contrast to circumspective
dealings. By clearly defining circumspective dealings with the ready-to-hand as
Dasein's primary and primordial relationship to beings, in *Being and Time* he held
knowledge of the present-at-hand to be a merely secondary and derivative relationship; now, on the other hand, precisely this relationship to the present-at-hand
comes forward as primordial and primary. And in an essay from 1928 this goes so far
that Heidegger now characterizes the primordial relationship to beings (which in
Being and Time he had understood exclusively as "Being alongside . . . the ready-to-
hand") solely as "Being alongside . . . the present-at-hand," and hence he simply
omits the "Being alongside . . . the ready-to-hand" which was previously primordial
("Vom Wesen des Grundes" *Wegmarke*, 2nd ed., p. 161 [*The Essence of Reasons*, pp.
101f.]).[5]

At the same time, as certain as the derivation of this now more positively valued
knowledge of the present-at-hand from its previously more negative evaluation may
be, it is just as certain that both are now to be carefully distinguished on account of
the differing evaluation given to each. For the change in evaluation is by no means
to be understood as meaning that Heidegger thereby simply drops his negative eval-

uation of knowledge of the present-at-hand. On the contrary, he holds to it and subjects it (particularly in its distinctive form as natural science) more and more to his well-known critique. He does so because from now on he sees increasingly the spontaneity of this knowledge of the present-at-hand, and so less and less does he see a difference between it and circumspection regarding the ready-to-hand.

This is precisely the reason why, from now on, not only knowledge of the present-at-hand (which was previously evaluated relatively negatively) but also circumspection regarding the ready-to-hand (which was previously valued entirely positively) come to be evaluated negatively. Behind this is nothing other than an insight that was staggering for Heidegger: human Dasein in fact always occurs as a "subjectivity of the subject," which from the start is oriented on success, but which in fact already shows its most extreme abuses in knowing as well as in natural science, not to mention in mere doing as well as in technology.

Only by bearing all this in mind can one see what is in store when, on the other hand, Heidegger once again begins to value this very knowledge of the present-at-hand more positively: that even knowing, which finally develops into natural science, can be understood only as the subject's intention to succeed, and hence that truth here can be understood only as the success and thus as the spontaneous achievement of the subjectivity of the subject—the actual magnitude of Dasein's practicism shocks Heidegger to such an extent that he recoils from it and instead retreats completely, toward a theoreticism.

What he, as it were, cleaves off from "theoretical" knowledge of the present-at-hand (which he had previously evaluated negatively in relation to "practical" circumspection regarding the ready-to-hand), and thus now makes independent as a separate and now positively valued knowledge of the present-at-hand, is none other than the characteristic of Aristotelian θεωρία which was supposed to apply to it in the first place, but which now can no longer do so. The fact that knowing, whose spontaneity develops not only into natural science but finally into technology as well, consists solely in a receptive "perceiving" of beings, and hence also that the truth of such knowing occurs only as the "unconcealedness" of beings themselves which is perceived with it—all this is now seen as a mere appearance.[6] Heidegger now takes back all of these characteristics of θεωρία and claims that together they comprise something fundamentally different; and immediately after *Being and Time* he presents this as a knowledge of the present-at-hand, which has been revalued as something entirely positive.[7]

The chronological beginning as well as the substantive and systematic principle of what Heidegger attempts to set forth as the actual essence of human beings, as opposed to any subjectivity in knowing and doing or natural science and technology, lies precisely in this. In the end Heidegger conceives this authentic essence—which human beings can find, on his view, only in a "step back," and this means in a step prior to knowing and doing—so extremely, as a receptive θεωρία, that it thereby becomes fundamentally questionable whether such a return can be an issue for human beings at all.[8]

For however this may best be understood, the primary question here is whether this most extreme invasion of antiquity into modernity and the present (an invasion which appears already in *Being and Time* as a reappropriation of knowing as "perception" [νόησις] and of truth as "unconcealedness" [ἀ-λήθεια]) does not in the end lead the late Heidegger into something quite utopian—and does this not indeed lead him into a utopian backwardness in the chronological as well as the substantive and systematic respects?

Now, if it is correct that even the most primordial perception of something constitutes just such a case of knowing, in which subjectivity is oriented on success simply in order by means of it to be further oriented on success in doing, then the question arises: how could something prior to such perception possibly be more primordial than subjectivity and still be human? Not only the perception of a "jug" (systematically speaking) but also the perception of a "presocratic" (chronologically speaking) always already has just this character of the "subjectivity" of the human subject; and what in fact may have arisen only in the modern age is simply a reflection on this. What simply cannot be ignored here is what a "step" before such perception and subjectivity could possibly lead "back" to, if not to their dissolution and hence to the dissolution of human being itself.

It is important to bear this in mind, since one could easily arrive at the idea that, with this θεωρία transposed into a utopian backwardness, the late Heidegger departs from the aforementioned practicism, and that he avoids it not in the direction of a utopian theoreticism but instead in the direction of a completely nonutopian aestheticism. Such an interpretation would seem even more fitting given that after *Being and Time* Heidegger not only turns very penetratingly to the theme of art but also often employs, in his retreat from practicism, an aestheticizing mode of expression.

Nonetheless, such an interpretation would be mistaken, because that "step back"—if one takes literally what Heidegger has in mind here—would have to preclude from the start any aesthetic attitude on the part of humans toward beings. For even if the theories about this attitude differ from one another in many ways, they all still agree on one thing: an aesthetic attitude always has perception and hence knowing as its foundation, and this is a conclusion that Heidegger wants to avoid.

Now, the question whether and how something like an aesthetic attitude toward what is perceived is at all possible arises because the perception of what is perceived always does in fact have just that sense that Heidegger wants to avoid. Even in primordial perception, in which it first acquires beings as in each case what is perceived, Dasein is in the aforementioned sense practically oriented subjectivity; in this, Dasein has from the start *practical* satisfaction or *practical* revulsion, an attitude that gets expressed in formulations like "this tree is useful for . . ." or is harmful for. . . ." Only because of this does the problem then arise whether and how such subjectivity can have a *non*practical ("indifferent") satisfaction or a *non*practical ("indifferent") revulsion rather than a practical one, in regard to what is perceived; such an attitude would then get expressed in formulations like "this tree is beautiful" or ". . . is ugly." For even this latter kind of attitude toward beings must in each case have as its basis the attitude "this tree . . ." and hence the perception "this is a tree. . . ."

If such an aesthetic attitude is supposed to be possible not simply in spite of the aforementioned attitude but rather precisely on the basis of it, then in no case can this occur through subjectivity's going back to a point prior to the perceiving that goes on in that aesthetic attitude. For it would thereby lose what is perceived, and with it everything that this attitude must first of all find, just in order to find what is perceived to be beautiful or ugly. Such an aesthetic attitude can, on the contrary, be possible only in virtue of subjectivity's going *beyond* perceiving, since, in connection with the achievement which it has always already produced with this perception, it always produces at least one additional achievement, namely, to *deny* itself any further practical purpose by means of this perceiving and, nonetheless, at the same time to complete this very perceiving. For this, either less subjectivity or none at all, as Heidegger has in mind, is by no means necessary; rather, what is necessary is more of it, because for this, nothing less is necessary than that subjectivity fundamentally overcome subjectivity and hence itself—an achievement that demands something extreme of subjectivity.

NOTES

1. To say nothing of the fact that it would still also have to be possible to say of such a being itself, for example, of some wood, that it is *true or false*. Thus even Heidegger, as we have recently come to know from the collected edition of his works, undertook in connection with the project of *Being and Time* a comprehensive attempt to develop a conception of falsity corresponding to this conception of truth— an attempt in which he evidently failed, as did Aristotle, from whom he took his point of departure

in this connection (cf. Heidegger, *Logik: Die Frage nach der Wahrheit, Gesamtausgabe,* Vol. 21 [Frank-furt: Klostermann, 1976], sections 13–16). This very fact might be the reason why in *Being and Time* itself Heidegger maintains only very rarely and in passing that this conception applies correspondingly to falsity as well (cf. p. 62), which is nonetheless not at all intelligible (cf. above pp. 16f.).

2. Cf., e.g., Ernst Tugendhat, *Der Wahrheitsbegriff bei Husserl und Heidegger* 2nd ed. (Berlin: De Gruyter, 1970), pp. 371ff.

3. Cf, e.g., Gottlob Frege, *Kleine Schriften,* ed. Ignacio Angelelli (Darmstadt: Wissenschaftliche Buchge-sellschaft, 1967), pp. 343f.

4. That this does not become fully clear here is due primarily to the fact that in several passages Hei-degger again considers Dasein as being "for its own sake" (cf., e.g., *Wegmarken,* 2nd ed. [Frankfurt: Klostermann, 1978], pp. 129f, 154f, 161; *The Essence of Reasons,* bilingual ed., trans. Terence Malick [Evanston: Northwestern University Press, 1969], pp. 21ff., 81ff., 101ff.), in which according to *Being and Time* Dasein's most primordial relationship to beings, as "ready-to-hand equipment" in the "envi-ronment," has its final ground. Hence such passages easily give rise to the appearance that in this regard Heidegger might still occupy exactly the same standpoint as in *Being and Time.* But inasmuch as he now plays down just this "environment" of "equipment" and would like to deny in principle that these are the primordial beings for Dasein, this "for the sake of" finally loses its concreteness as well as its function and gets left behind as a mere abstraction, which Heidegger subsequently does not dis-cuss further.

5. Shortly thereafter he avoids what is conspicuous in such an explicit omission by saying simply that "Dasein and beings without the character of Dasein" stand in this primordial relationship (*Wegmarken,* 2nd ed., p. 163 [*The Essence of Reasons,* p. 107]).

6. Accordingly, "observing" (*Betrachten*), which as a characterization of knowing the present-at-hand still had the sense of receptivity in *Being and Time,* now gets reinterpreted as something entirely sponta-neous. Heidegger now understands it in the sense of "striving" (*trachten*) as an "observing that strives after" (*Be-trachten*) in the sense of "treating or refining," as in the Latin *tractare.* Cf. "Wissenschaft und Besinnung," *Vorträge und Aufsätze,* 4th ed. (Pfullingen: Neske, 1978), p. 52 ["Science and Reflection," *The Question Concerning Technology and Other Essays,* trans. William Lovitt (New York: Harper and Row, 1977), p. 167]: "Modern science as theory in the sense of an observing that strives after is a refining of the real that does encroach uncannily upon it."

7. Later he characterizes it as a "thinking," which, as "responding and recalling" (*andenkendes*) or "reflec-tive" (*bedenkendes*) or "corresponding" (*entsprechendes*) thinking, is nevertheless supposed to be some-thing fundamentally different than "representational" or "explicative" thinking; instead he now des-ignates the negatively evaluated knowledge of the present-at-hand, and in particular natural science, by means of such expressions. That this nonetheless follows solely from a positive revaluation of knowl-edge of the present-at-hand is very clear from the fact that "things" are supposed "to come to" this thinking, things which are now valued in an entirely positive way, while earlier in *Being and Time* they were evaluated negatively as "mere things" in the sense of "merely present-at-hand objects for knowl-edge," in contrast with "ready-to-hand equipment." On this cf. "Das Ding," *Vorträge und Aufsätze,* 4th ed., e.g., pp. 159f., 169f., 174, 176, 178 ["The Thing," *Poetry, Language, Thought,* trans. Albert Hof-stadter (New York: Harper Colophon, 1971), pp. 167f., 176ff., 181, 183f., 184f.].

8. Cf., e.g., "The step back takes up its residence in a co-responding which, appealed to in the world's being by the world's being, answers within itself to that appeal. . . . When and in what way do things appear as things? They do not appear *by means of* human making. But neither do they appear without the vigilance of mortals. The first step toward such vigilance is the step back from the thinking that

merely represents—that is, explains . . ." ("Das Ding," p. 174 ["The Thing," pp. 181f]). "Man can represent, no matter how, only what has previously come to light of its own accord and has shown itself to him in the light it brought with it" ("Das Ding," p. 163 ["The Thing," p. 171]; cf. further "Wissenschaft und Besinnung," pp. 47f. ("Science and Reflection," pp. 162ff.]). To say nothing of the deep and never resolved ambiguity of the late Heidegger, on the basis of which not only what is positive in θεωρία, but also ultimately what is negative in knowing and doing, all actually go back to the essence either of human being itself or of something else.

7.

Materialism and Morality

It has now become clear that the aesthetic attitude of human being requires an *intensification* of human subjectivity for the sake of a determinate kind of self-overcoming. It follows from this that the "step" through which, on Heidegger's view, human beings can find their way from their subjectivity "back" to their authentic essence cannot be understood as an aestheticism at all; rather, as a theoreticism which is in fact utopian, it must finally remain unintelligible. Only by bearing this in mind can one make sense of the fact that Heidegger, whose reaction to practicism is to recoil from it, does not even consider the prospect of facing up to practicism, so as to confront subjectivity (which he quite rightly sees at work in this practicism) with the question of morality. Heidegger's insight into practicism penetrates so deeply that his alarm concerning it—namely, concerning subjectivity's obsession with success, the abysmal hideousness of which cannot be denied—turns into a desperation over subjectivity as such: Heidegger sees its excesses as obsession, but also as something natural (*Naturwüchsigkeit*)[1] that must either forge ahead (in whatever direction it happens to be going) or else come to a complete standstill.

Evidently Heidegger now fails to see that this obsession with success, in all its hideous magnitude, does not appear straightforwardly in human beings, as if it were something natural to which we could simply consign ourselves. This was familiar to him as the idea of human moral obligation and also as the idea of an aesthetic attitude in human beings, and not in name only. Both of these were also familiar to him as the idea of a specifically human possibility that enables subjectivity to exist in an entirely different way, since despite its obsession with success subjectivity is always fundamentally capable of bifurcating itself (*sich zu brechen*), thereby overcoming its mere naturalness.

But simply acknowledging this as a possibility would have forced Heidegger to acknowledge something positive in subjectivity beyond everything negative in it, and hence to abandon his exclusively negative evaluation of it. This in turn would necessarily have amounted to taking up once again the difficult discussion of the

57

complicated problem of subjectivity, which broke off after Kant and the German Idealists.

And yet this is precisely what does *not* occur.

From the fact that (e.g.) moral philosophy and aesthetics, which are practically absent in the earlier Heidegger, are also missing in the later Heidegger,[2] it is clear that Heidegger breaks off the discussion of subjectivity he had scarcely even begun in *Being and Time*; against the positive possibilities of human subjectivity that these disciplines once attempted to develop, he finally decides to evaluate anything like subjectivity in a wholly negative fashion.

With this decision Heidegger ends up aligning himself with those who, by breaking with Kant and the Idealists, have been able to think only as "materialists," and hence to this day have been able to think of subjectivity only as something straightforwardly natural. And yet a decision in favor of this all-too-simple understanding of the world and the self is particularly problematic for Heidegger, since in this very century it would have been in his power (though it is not in the materialists' power) to protect the subjectivity of human Dasein from this disastrous self-understanding.

In this regard it is important to realize that it is this decision (and not, as might appear to be the case, the practicism resulting from *Being and Time*) that aligns the later Heidegger on the side of the materialists.

That, from the viewpoint of the materialists, human subjectivity's obsession with success must in fact be conceived as something straightforwardly natural becomes clear especially in their conviction that even knowing, through which subjectivity aims at doing, and science, through which it proceeds toward technology, are themselves nothing but the expressions of an entirely "subjective interest" in knowledge (as doing and technology are); therefore, knowing and science are fundamentally subject to arbitrariness or even utter caprice. For just this reason all "objectivity" and "objective truth" claimed by subjectivity for knowledge and science are seen either as a mere illusion, in which subjectivity overextends itself, or else as an ideology of subjectivity, in which it strives to veil what is merely subjective in knowledge and science.

As is now well known, adherents of "critical theory" came forward with this conviction and ended up in a controversy, still unsettled, with adherents of "critical rationalism."[3] And at first glance one could easily get the impression that if Heidegger himself had developed a practicism on the basis of *Being and Time*, it would have led him to side with "critical theory."

For in the end such a practicism results in a primacy of doing and practice over knowing and theory, because subjectivity intends something like knowing and theory only on the basis of an intention oriented on doing and practice—and does this not amount to saying that knowing is every bit as subjective as doing?

But upon closer inspection it becomes clear that there can be no such talk. If one keeps in view the precise sense in which doing enjoys this primacy over knowing, then it becomes clear that such a practicism would lead Heidegger to side with neither "critical theory" nor "critical rationalism." In contrast with both he would really have reached a standpoint of his own, which would have enabled him to be the first to settle, in a truly "critical" fashion, those aspects of the controversy which remain unsettled.

Controversy arises about these ideas only because, when it comes to knowing and doing, these positions distinguish neither between noesis and noema nor between poiesis and poiema. And, of course, the disputes arising in this connection cannot be settled as long as these fundamental distinctions are observed.

Now, if it is right that in general subjectivity intends knowing solely because doing (toward which it ultimately aims) can be intended only on the basis of knowing, then surely the representatives of "critical theory" are not entirely wrong. In virtue of this primacy of doing over knowing (and that means in virtue of the dependence of knowing on doing), knowing, just like doing, is something which is subjective through and through—but exclusively in the noetic-poietic sense, as an *act* of knowledge or an *act* of doing (*Handlungsakt*). Representatives of "critical theory" go wrong only because, in lacking that distinction, they are led to conceive such subjective knowing (as well as doing) in the noematic-poiematic sense, as something subjective.

For even if subjectivity should be so subjective in its activity as to be arbitrary, with respect to the poiema (toward which it always shapes its subjective poiesis) it is directed not toward this poiema as such but rather toward it only in order to be successful in doing. But for precisely this reason it must, as subjectivity, renounce all arbitrariness with respect to poiema and noema and be utterly objective rather than subjective. In order to be successful, it must not only direct its poiema in doing entirely in accordance with the noema of the relevant knowing; above all it must proceed with this noema in knowing toward success, and this means toward objective truth about actuality itself. For only thus can it attempt, having successful doing in view, to change reality so that something not yet actual might become actual.

As something subjective, noesis therefore depends on poiesis because, given the success toward which subjectivity is striving here, the poiema conversely depends on the noema as something objective. Nothing changes with respect to this noematic objectivity of knowing if, instead of success (toward which subjectivity always strives in connection with a noema), subjectivity encounters failure: where error occurs knowing then becomes not objectively true but instead objectively *false*. Such objectivity in knowing—whether, factually, subjectivity now finds itself in truth or in error—must form the basis for all of subjectivity's activity, but especially when subjectivity would like to succeed in its more complex activities, for example, in "lying" or in "repression" or "ideology."

But given this, one simply cannot say that the practicism of Heidegger's *Being and Time* entails a conception of subjectivity as something straightforwardly natural. On the contrary, this practicism leads instead to the following insight: precisely as that obsession with success which awakens this impression of something straightforwardly natural, from the start subjectivity is always essentially something bifurcated. As obsessed with success as it may be when it acts, and as subjective or even arbitrary as it may be in its orientation toward success—precisely for this reason subjectivity must from the start be bifurcated when it acts, since for all the arbitrariness in its subjective activity, it still submits itself to objective knowing, and that means to the very actuality at which it must always arrive in successful knowing if it is to be successful in doing.

As just such an *activity* obsessed with success, something like subjectivity is simply *not* straightforwardly natural; instead, from the start it is bifurcated into *knowing and* doing. Indeed, subjectivity can move beyond its bifurcated nature so deeply into objective knowing that the impression easily arises that, at least in such cases, knowing arises solely for its own sake and not for the sake of doing; that is, the impression easily arises that at least in such cases there is no primacy of doing over knowing, no noetic-poietic dependence of knowing on doing, but instead that at least here knowing is independent of doing.

But this impression could be due to a mistake arising in the following way. From the fact that for one specific kind of doing (e.g., for technology) only one specific kind of knowing (e.g., natural science) is the "substantively relevant" (*inhaltlich relevant*) knowing, one can easily be led to the mistaken conclusion that by the same token one specific kind of knowing (e.g., natural science) is the "substantively relevant" knowing only for one specific kind of doing (e.g., for technology).

But this does not follow at all. It is by no means certain, simply from the content (*Inhalt*) of a specific cognition, which activity that knowing is "substantively relevant" for. If, for instance, a natural scientist pursues natural science not for technological purposes but instead for the sake of satisfying a need that may be merely his own, then for *this* activity on the part of subjectivity natural science is the "substantively relevant" knowing.

This leads to more than just the question about what pursuing natural science "for its own sake" is really supposed to mean. In particular, it becomes questionable whether it is possible in general for human beings to pursue something like knowledge as an "end in itself," whether for such subjectivity something like θεωρία is in fact entirely utopian, rather than simply being a kind of regression (as Heidegger would have it).[4]

But even this would not change the fact that such subjectivity, even if in its knowing it always aims toward doing, invariably bifurcates its fundamental intention toward *doing* into the intention toward *knowing and doing*; moreover, this would not change the fact that, however subjective it may be in the latter (perhaps even to the point of peculiarity), it is objective to the same extent in the former.

Given this insight Heidegger would have been able, on the basis of the practicism of *Being and Time*, to reinitiate the discussion of the "subjectivity of the subject" that broke off after Kant and the Idealists, and to carry it further. For on the basis of the insight that from the start, *a priori*, subjectivity does and must place itself *at a distance* from its intention toward doing and hence from itself as an identity, into the difference between knowing and doing, and on the basis of the insight that with knowing and doing subjectivity does and must come to stand in a most extreme difference *opposed* to all others within this whole, Heidegger would have been able to maintain in its essentials and to develop further the differentiated human understanding of world and self that the Idealists had already developed. In contrast with those materialists who would simply like to replace this complex and difficult human understanding of world and self with their simpler one, Heidegger's insight would not have been of merely theoretical interest but above all would have been of practical interest as well.

For it would have offered probably the best prospect so far for investigating whether the moral law—which Kant had to leave behind as simply an underived "fact of reason" after his attempt to derive it failed[5]—might be derivable after all and thus might finally be secured against the suspicion of illusion or even of ideology. For the insight, that subjectivity must first of all bifurcate its intention toward doing into an intention toward *knowing and* doing, would at least have strongly suggested the idea that even the moral law, on the basis of which subjectivity more specifically bifurcates itself in its activity, constitutes only a special case of its bifurcation into knowing and doing.

This viewpoint could have done more than save Heidegger (i) from understanding something like subjectivity, simply because of its obsession with success, as something straightforwardly natural (thereby agreeing with the materialists), and (ii) from fleeing in desperation into utopian regression. This viewpoint would have put him, even in the twentieth century, in a position to show all those materialists—those who know no such desperation, and who instead of fleeing despondently backward march energetically forward—what is utopian but also disastrous in such a forward movement. For there is an obvious difficulty for these materialists: instead of attributing to subjectivity (which is obsessed with success) mastery in the sense of a total manipulation based on particular successful manipulations, these materialists attribute to subjectivity mastery in a different sense—and thus they fail to see the prospect of permanent catastrophe.

Notes

1. On this see, for example, his characterization of subjectivity as *Homo animalis* in contrast with *Homo humanus*, which according to Heidegger can come to be only through that "step back," understood here as a "descent" from a "subjectivity which has strayed" ("Brief über den 'Humanismus,'" *Wegmarken*, 2nd ed. (Frankfurt: Klostermann, 1978), pp. 348f ["Letter on Humanism," *Basic Writings*, rev. ed., ed. David Farrell Krell (San Francisco: Harper and Row, 1993), p. 254]).

2. Even the parts of *Being and Time* in which Heidegger comes to speak of phenomena like "conscience" and "guilt" (cf. ¶¶54–60) can hardly be counted as counterexamples to this. For on closer examination it could be demonstrated that Heidegger here substantially a-moralizes (*entmoralisiert*) these phenomena through his treatment of them. Therefore, it is also quite legitimate that shortly after the appearance of *Being and Time* Heidegger was asked the question, "When will you write an ethics?" But even the way in which he later refers to and considers this question is sufficient to illuminate how unprepared he is to let something like "ethics" count as a positive undertaking. For he is finally able to see even in something like an "ethical" attitude of subjectivity only a very thoroughly organized form of subjectivity's obsession with success. (Cf. "Brief über den 'Humanismus,'" pp. 349ff. ["Letter on Humanism," pp. 254ff.])

3. Regarding this controversy, see in particular the position of Elisabeth Ströker in her *Einführung in die Wissenschaftstheorie* (Darmstadt: Wissenschaftliche Buchgesellschaft, 1973), pp. 117ff.

4. It is precisely in this respect that the representatives of "critical rationalism," who rightly want to hold on to the objectivity of knowing, run the risk of going wrong. In order to be able to maintain this objectivity, they think that they must also insist that knowing can arise altogether independently of doing, and hence that it is not dependent on doing even in the noetic-poietic sense—hence that it is not subjective. Thus, for example, as Elisabeth Ströker appropriately puts it, the representatives of "critical rationalism" are of the opinion "that a certain amount of adequately secured knowing is necessary *in order to constitute interests*" (*Einführung in die Wissenschaftstheorie*, p. 130, emphasis mine). But with this opinion they not only go wrong, they also open themselves up to repeated objections from representatives of "critical theory," thereby making what is wrong appear right; and then the entire dispute between them reaches an impasse.

5. Immanuel Kant, *Kritik der praktischen Vernunft, Kants gesammelte Schriften*, Akademie Ausgabe (Berlin: De Gruyter, 1902–), Vol. V, cf. p. 31 with p. 91.

Heidegger and Practical Philosophy

"We are still far from pondering the essence of action (*Handelns*) decisively enough"—with this assertion Heidegger begins his "Letter on Humanism."[1] This assertion, however, will initially mislead every reader who considers it against the background of *Being and Time*. It can only lead the reader to expect that the distinctive elements contained in that work and in Western philosophy leading up to it will be developed into a general theory of action, one that takes action as such as its theme prior to a consideration of any questions concerning the morality or the ethics of action. In any event this assertion leads one to expect that Heidegger will develop a Practical Philosophy, if not in the sense just stated then at least in the sense of a theory of the morality or the ethics of action, an endeavor to which *Being and Time* makes hardly any contribution whatsoever.

It must then come as a complete shock to every such reader when it becomes apparent that this very assertion leads one into the context of a thinking that has long worked in bitter opposition to any Practical Philosophy conceived as a theoretical discipline; this opposition has no equal anywhere in Western philosophy.[2] For by the time of the "Letter on Humanism" there had long since ceased to be any talk in Heidegger of such Practical Philosophy—either of a retrieval of a moral theory or ethics, or even of a refinement of a theory of action that had first been presented in *Being and Time*. The question posed to him ("soon after" this work had appeared), "When are you going write an ethics?" now gets discussed by Heidegger as if the "young friend" who posed the question had been able to infer quite clearly simply on the basis of *Being and Time* that the question may rest on a fundamental misunderstanding.[3] Accordingly, shortly after *Being and Time* Heidegger wants, if at all possible, to have nothing more to do with it. In that work he himself developed the discipline of a general theory of action much further, and disclosed the dimension of human action as such more fundamentally, than all of his predecessors in Western philosophy taken together.

At the same time, in *Being and Time* he arrived at the decisive insight that the fundamental structure of human Dasein is the practical structure of "care," which pertains to that being for which "in its very Being, that Being is an issue for it"[4]—a structure that Heidegger uncovers, as is well known, by taking as his point of departure Kant's concept of human beings as "ends in themselves," a concept which in the first instance is morally neutral.[5] Above all, what was most decisive in this insight was that from out of just this fundamental structure of "care"—which ultimately gets named by the tautology "care for oneself"[6]—human Dasein approaches all other beings, that is, those lacking the character of Dasein, first of all in the mode of practical "concern." On this basis such beings are always primarily "ready-to-hand equipment" for practical "dealings"; they are never simply "present-at-hand things" that serve as "objects" for theoretical "knowledge," but instead can become so only subsequently, namely, through a change in human Dasein's attitude toward them.[7]

After *Being and Time*, however, Heidegger moves progressively further away from this orientation, which is one of the most original and promising things presented there. The essay "The Essence of Reasons" includes a great many passages where the matter under consideration ("Being-in-the-world," "intentionality" as "transcendence") would really require him to come back to the primary Being of the readiness-to-hand of beings as equipment for Dasein's practical dealings, and yet his failure to do so is conspicuous. Even where he cannot avoid mentioning it, he leaves aside what is decisive, namely, the primacy of the readiness-to-hand of equipment and the corresponding primacy of practical dealings, and he plays down the entire "analysis of the environment": it remains "of subordinate significance" because it simply "prepares the way" and "leads over" to an authentic analysis of "world" and "Being-in-the-world."[8]

Already, only a few years after *Being and Time*, he no longer wants to accept the obvious implications of this. For here Heidegger starts to exhibit an antagonism that is aimed only secondarily at Practical Philosophy because it is aimed primarily at human practice or action; this antagonism becomes increasingly evident,[9] and its bitterness is related in an odd way to its futility. Indeed, it is directed toward nothing less than the innermost essence of the subjectivity of the subject; Heidegger's extensive philosophical analysis of this notion in *Being and Time* succeeded in such a manner that he subsequently strove toward an even more fundamental destruction of it.

Hence the answer to the question concerning the basis for this antagonism can only be found in *Being and Time*. Something must have occurred in this work whose consequences shook Heidegger and moved him to this reversal, as dramatic as it was radical, as soon as he saw them.

It is in precisely the respect mentioned above that Heidegger, in *Being and Time*, was the first to re-enter the sequence of great endeavors extending from Kant to

Hegel. Once again he urgently pursues the central question of the relationship between human knowing and doing, or theory and practice, which occupied a central place for those thinkers. But in advocating the primacy of doing or practice over knowing or theory even more decisively than they had, he gets caught up in much deeper difficulties than they had. For even if human Dasein, understood as "concern," may primarily be practical, active "dealings" with beings that are "ready-to-hand equipment," and is only in a secondary sense the theoretical, knowing "objectification" of such beings to mere "present-at-hand things," such dealings certainly do not proceed blindly: for example, to hammer with a hammer, one must first perceive it. Nonetheless, such perception is not supposed to be a theoretical knowledge of things, but instead is supposed to be practical "circumspection" regarding equipment. This is a first difficulty, which has a second one as its flip-side: even theoretical knowing, in particular natural science, is in principle supposed to be "concern," and hence even it must have practical import. Heidegger gives as an example of this the use of microscopes.[10] But this does not suffice for what Heidegger has in mind here. For even circumspection in connection with hammering is not supposed to be practical on account of, say, Dasein's wearing glasses when it does so. Theory itself is supposed to be practical in itself, rather than being so simply on account of the fact that practice goes along with it.

If one investigates this difficulty further, a surprising result becomes apparent: in *Being and Time*, Heidegger is unable to designate anything else as the practical import of theory. For he conceives the theoretical knowing of the present-at-hand—and thus natural science as the distinctive case of such knowing—entirely in the sense of Aristotelian θεωρία, namely, as a "pure perceiving of" or "mute tarrying alongside" beings,[11] in which human beings in no way aim at doing or practice; in such cases theory, to the extent that it is purposive at all, is itself the purpose.

It is precisely here that Heidegger's reversal after *Being and Time* becomes completely clear. Only after this work does he come (indeed all the more rapidly and decisively) to his insight into the real essence of knowledge and natural science. But this new insight now leads to an assessment of knowledge and natural science that is the exact opposite of their assessment in *Being and Time*; and it ultimately leads to a revision of the very foundations of that work, a revision that would have required a reconceiving of that work from the ground up. Knowledge and natural science, it is said later, are, as theory, "a refining of the real that does encroach uncannily upon it";[12] as theory, they are a kind of practice that at bottom simply develops into the practice of technology.

It is technology in this sense that becomes the impetus for the reversal in Heidegger's thinking. And the fundamental character of Heidegger's turn away from

Being and Time on the basis of this insight is patently evident from the following: in that work, technology in this sense is never mentioned once, and this is no accident. That it is neither named nor dealt with substantively in *Being and Time*, and that it cannot be, is due to the fact that natural science, conceived in the sense of Aristotelian θεωρία, possesses no affinity whatsoever with technology in this sense. The essential connection between the two, and ultimately their essential sameness, was not yet apparent to the Heidegger of *Being and Time*. In this work there can be no talk of the fact that technology might appear to be the mere extension of natural science, but ultimately reveals itself to be the proper essence of the latter. It must have deeply dismayed Heidegger when he finally discovered these two things at once: the thoroughly technological, that is, practical, essence even of "theoretical" knowledge as the "objectification" of beings as "present-at-hand things," particularly in natural science; and, together with this, the obvious lack of an insight into that essence in *Being and Time*.

Heidegger's dismay must have been deepened by the further insight (which was made inevitable by these discoveries) that natural science, whose essence is technology and hence practice, can no longer, as had been thought in *Being and Time*, be the distinctive case of theoretical "knowledge of present-at-hand things" but must instead be the distinctive case of practical "circumspection regarding ready-to-hand equipment"—and hence it is the distinctive case of what had been presented in *Being and Time*, in a positive light and with no qualification whatsoever, as human Dasein's authentically primordial access to other beings, a mode of access that is prior to all other modes. But with this Heidegger found himself in a unique position to make a crucial decision. For he had a distinctive opportunity here, namely, to transform his dismay into a self-critique; in doing so, he could have shown that the relationship between theory and practice that he had developed in *Being and Time* is untenable for reasons that follow from the very subject matter, and that these reasons find expression in difficulties that arise already in that work.

According to *Being and Time*, theoretical knowledge of the present-at-hand and practical circumspection regarding the ready-to-hand are so fundamentally different that in each case the move from the latter to the former is effected only through a "change-over."[13] Theory in this sense is said to possess the fundamental form of predication, so that in each case Dasein can be "in the truth"[14] and hence can also be in falsity. But then it would also have to be the case that circumspection cannot yet possess the character of being true or false. In fact, according to Heidegger circumspection is not predicative at all but instead is "pre-predicative."[15] But with this he contradicts himself in *Being and Time* itself, since he must admit there that even circumspection, which he takes to be primordial perception of beings in the environment,[16] can "go wrong";[17] hence not only can circumspection be true, but it can also be false in cases involving an error in perception. This is but one of a number of points in *Being and Time* that make it clear that Heidegger fails in his attempt to draw a sharp distinction between practical circumspection regarding the ready-to-hand and theoretical knowledge of the present-at-hand. At least to the extent that it can be true or false, practical circumspection itself must already be theoretical knowledge.

At the same time, the converse follows from this as a truly significant consequence. Just like circumspection, theoretical knowing, which begins with primordial perception of beings and continues into mature natural science, must itself be practical knowing. In fact, following his dismaying insight, Heidegger himself could have worked this out in the course of a self-critique by radicalizing his theory of "concern." For as he shows in *Being and Time*,[18] concern can occur as "disturbed," so that in principle it can be either undisturbed or disturbed. This means that, as "Being directed toward" something definite,[19] concern can attain or fall short of this definite something and hence can be a success or a failure, that is, it can lead to a success or a failure on the part of concernful Dasein. But Heidegger could have radicalized this—indeed he should have, since it holds not only for concern understood as doing, to which he limited it in *Being and Time*, but equally for concern understood as knowing. In all the instances considered in *Being and Time*, that which disturbs is discovered in each case *as* that which disturbs; this means that the circumspection which guides is always posited as undisturbed, and it thereby protects action from failing even more seriously. But then Heidegger would have to admit that circumspective knowing can also be "disturbed": first, because he takes circumspection to be an instance of concern that can be "disturbed"; and second, because he believes that in fact circumspection can also "go wrong."

But this would then mean that even circumspective knowing is a "Being directed toward" something definite, and that as such it can succeed or fail, that is, it can lead to a success or a failure on the part of concernful Dasein. Such failure in knowing, however, is nothing other than the falsity of knowing. Consequently, truth would be nothing other than success in knowing. And in fact, just as in principle concernful Dasein never aims at failure in doing but rather only at success, in principle it also never aims at failure in knowing, that is, at falsity, but rather only at success, that is, at truth. Hence in knowing, just as in doing, if a failure should occur, then in principle it can only count as something that does no more than interfere with a concernful Dasein's fundamental intention to succeed: in knowledge, which in principle is the intention to arrive at truth, falsity can occur only as unintended falsity, that is, it can interfere only in the form of error.

If this unanticipated insight had so dismayed Heidegger that he had articulated a self-critique and a radicalization of his theory of concern, then he would have developed a theory of the subjectivity of the subject surpassing any such theory that had yet been offered by modernity: not only doing but even knowing is nothing other than the intention to succeed on the part of human Dasein as a subject; and accordingly, falsity is nothing but failure and truth nothing but success on the part of this knowing subject. The subjectivity of the subject would thus have come to light as a thoroughgoing practicity (*Praktizität*) the extent of which had never before been known. Such practicity would be plausible because subjectivity intends truth as success in knowing just in order to achieve success in doing, which is what subjectivity is authentically directed toward. For in fact, it is only on the basis of a successfully known environment that it is possible for subjectivity in that environment to act successfully, whether hammering with a hammer or flying in a rocket. Such a thoroughly developed theory of "circumspection" regarding "ready-to-hand equipment" in the "environment" was only barely anticipated in modernity by the German Idealists after Kant.

As stated above, all this was already sketched out in *Being and Time* and, in accordance with the insight discussed above, would have been easy for a thinker like Heidegger to develop. This insight into the practicity of the subjectivity of the subject underlies his later critique of natural science and technology, though it remained undeveloped because he evaluated it negatively. A positive evaluation of practicity would have permitted Heidegger to develop a positive theory of the subjectivity of the subject as well, thereby extending modernity in a constructive manner; but he was unable to commit himself to such a positive evaluation, for reasons that can only be guessed at.

One guess is that at least one of these reasons had to do with unfortunate historical circumstances. A thinker like Heidegger, whose most fundamental schooling was in ancient and medieval philosophy, must initially have been repelled by the philosophizing of anything like Neo-Kantianism; and this must have kept him from using his study of Neo-Kantianism, as well as of Kant and his followers, to work out his own view. In any event, all available sources suggest that Heidegger's most penetrating engagement and confrontation with Kantian and post-Kantian philosophy began only after the position of *Being and Time* had been firmly established. But in the sections of this work that deal with the theory of knowledge, Heidegger shows himself to be entirely predisposed toward medieval-ancient concepts, which held sway over him for two reasons—primarily because of his own studies, but also because of those of Brentano and Husserl.

The problem with Heidegger's mature interpretation of Kant is not that it onesidedly understands Kant's philosophy in ontological terms: Heidegger is justifiably opposed to the onesidedness of the Neo-Kantians, who understood Kant exclusively in epistemological terms; and up to the present he has been contributing to a more balanced picture of Kant. Given the essential unity of epistemology and ontology in Kant, which Heidegger sees very clearly, the real problem with his interpretation of Kant is that he is unable to do justice, either epistemologically or ontologically, to Kant's Copernican turn.

This has been evident at least since 1975–76, when his Marburg lectures from the winter semester of 1925–26 and the summer semester of 1927 were published.[20] In these texts, long stretches of which exhibit the beginning of Heidegger's engagement and confrontation with Kant, it becomes particularly clear that Heidegger's discussion of Kant goes so far as to say that what Kant refers to merely as "spontaneity" really signifies "intentionality."[21]

From this it is quite clear just how fundamentally Heidegger fails to see the meaning of the Copernican turn, a meaning that Kant connects with spontaneity as the intentionality of subjectivity. Intentionality in the wholly medieval-ancient (i.e., pre-Copernican) sense, which passed from Brentano to Husserl and from Husserl onward, can, even on Heidegger's view,[22] be directed in principle only at something that must not simply already be real but must also, as what is real, already be "manifest," "disclosed," or "unconcealed."[23]

But Kant means precisely the opposite of this since, even if he does not use the word "intentionality," he stays closer to the relevant idea: in accordance with its real meaning, intentionality can in principle be directed not at something that is already actual, but rather only at something that it seeks to actualize; indeed, that at which it is directed becomes actual by means of intentionality itself. This is so essential a part of its fundamentally practical meaning that it would be meaningless, and superfluous, to intend something that is already actual, as this would amount to a *mere* "theoretical" knowing of something. On Kant's view, in principle theoretical knowing cannot be a mere objectification of something that is already actual, though this was the view of pre-Copernican epistemology as a theory of natural consciousness. On the contrary, knowing, just like doing, can only consist in the attempt to take something that has already been objectified (namely, by means of "constitutive mathematical" categories, schemata, and principles) and actualize it (namely, by means of merely "regulative dynamical" ones).[24] To the extent that objects in the external world are actual, they are never anything but our "products," that is, they are nothing but factical-contingent results of our intentionality. We have here, according to Kant, the only possible conception—that is, the only one that we can rationally develop—of empirical reality.

The Heidegger of *Being and Time* was already pressed toward a practicity of subjectivity understood as intentionality, one that is comparable to the one just discussed. He had already articulated an extensive theoretical conception of it and conferred on it an entirely positive status; in accordance with his later insight, he could have developed it even further in connection with technology—had this later insight not gotten in his way and become an obstacle that he was never able to overcome, presumably because he never tried to overcome it. For Heidegger after *Being and Time*, the fact that subjectivity, in the sense of intentionally structured practicity, has technology as its authentic essence, and the fact that this holds for all its knowing, becomes the decisive impetus for his reversal, which as we have seen gives rise to a wholly negative evaluation of subjectivity. The essence of subjectivity's knowing cannot consist in receptive *theoria*, that is, in "pure perceiving of" or "mute tarrying alongside" beings, and the essence of such beings can no longer consist in their "manifestness" or "unconcealedness" for such knowing; instead, the essence of both consists in technology, that is, ultimately in willing and its success—once this occurs to Heidegger, it becomes impossible for him to view the subjectivity of the subject in a positive light, and consequently it becomes impossible for him to develop the theory of subjectivity any further.

And not only that. To the extent that the only kind of tarrying-perceiving *theoria* that he is now able to view in a positive light is the human "thinking that responds and recalls"[25] that occurs in a "step back,"[26] namely, a step back from all subjectivity in knowing and doing,[27] Heidegger finally opts for an illegitimate antiquity over a legitimate modernity. Henceforth not only does Heidegger no longer place a positive value on a theoretical construction of subjectivity that would advance modernity, that is, on Practical Philosophy, under the rubric of which even Theoretical Philosophy would now have to come; henceforth what is at issue for him is an even more radical, though purely negative, destruction of subjectivity—*the practical being*—and this destruction would deprive practical philosophy of its very subject matter.

Now, in order to adhere to this exclusively negative evaluation of subjectivity, Heidegger has to pay a very high price, which he seems to have had little hesitation about paying: he abandons the idea that the active subject (*handelnder Subjekte*) has its own essence, and hence also the idea that the subject has a special place in contrast to objects, which bring about effects in a merely natural-causal manner. Modernity had struggled to argue for both of these ideas. Now Heidegger is able to adhere to this entirely negative evaluation of subjectivity only by being prepared to level the essential distinction between subject and object, by reducing subjectivity's activity to the mere bringing about of effects.

Although there is a great deal of evidence for this, we shall point out just a few particularly clear instances. "We are still far from pondering the essence of action decisively enough" is the beginning of the "Letter on Humanism," which was cited earlier and which has now been shown to be misleading. Heidegger then continues by saying, "We view action only as causing an effect."[28] Natural events, which are governed by causal laws, consist essentially in "causing an effect"; but this by itself does not mean that nature could be understood as something that acts (*handelnde*), that is, something that carries out intentions. Here Heidegger tacitly drops the requirement that causing an effect can count as intentional activity only if it origi- nates in an autonomous self-relation on the part of subjectivity, in contrast to the heteronomy of mere nature. It is in complete accord with this when a little later he explicitly reduces subjectivity to *Homo animalis*.[29] A human being, which as subjec- tivity knows and acts, is a mere "animal," just an animal among animals: "Animal drives and human *ratio* become identical."[30] So it can no longer be surprising that a substantive and objective assessment of technology simply cannot proceed from such an understanding of the human essence.

Of course, no one will deny that Heidegger deserves credit for having seen, early on and correctly, what is negative in technology.[31] Technology is a result of human endeavor, but it can no longer be maintained that the negative dimension of tech- nology is actually its essence; instead we can only consider whether the negativity of technology really consists in our having too much technology, or whether it might instead consist in our having too little technology, for example, too little to gain technological control over the undesirable side-effects of technology. For Heidegger, it has to be senseless to ask questions of this kind, because there is no one to whom they can be addressed, given that technology is ultimately nothing but a kind of wild, natural outgrowth of humanity; it is no different than the qualitative and quantitative hypertrophy of a beehive or an ant hill. But on the contrary, even the most hypertrophic technology is subjectivity to the extent that in technology sub- jectivity is practical, that is, subjectivity proceeds from its autonomy and seeks suc- cess intentionally, so that in each case it is mindful of something like a balance or a relationship between success and failure (or between end and means, result and expenditure, effect and side-effect, advantage and disadvantage). After Heidegger's reversal, none of this enters into consideration any more.

Heidegger's treatment of the question of ethics points in precisely the same direction. He does not really answer the question, but instead he dismisses it as a misunderstanding, offering in its place a superior view, one with as much perspec- tive as patience: "The desire for an ethics presses ever more ardently for fulfillment as the obvious no less than the hidden perplexity of man soars to immeasurable heights. The greatest care must be fostered upon the ethical bond at a time when technological man, delivered over to mass society, can be kept reliably on call only by gathering and ordering his plans and activities as a whole, in a way that corresponds to technology."[32] Here it is absolutely clear that Heidegger abjures the development of an ethics, simply because, in strict accordance with his negative conception of technology, all he can see in ethics is a super-technology that "corresponds to technology": a hypertrophic beehive or anthill that has no bearings and is bursting at the seams can ultimately be controlled ("be kept reliably on call") only in a totalitarian manner ("as a whole"), through techniques of social manipulation ("by gathering and ordering his plans and activities . . . in a way that corresponds to technology"). But here there is no longer any talk of the fact that even technological, hypertrophic subjectivity *is subjectivity*, not only to the extent that its foundational autonomy, structured in terms of intentionality, is concerned with success, but also to the extent that moral autonomy is concerned with restraining one's intentionality and with mastering one's lust for success.

Instead, Heidegger now speaks in favor of a "step back" into "thinking that responds and recalls," which as *ethos* has priority over all ethics, as the priority of a special kind of activity.[33] And this alone is what *Homo humanus*, in contrast to *Homo animalis*, consists in.[34] But with this Heidegger renders himself unable to give a comprehensible and useful answer to the question of what *Homo* as *humanus* is or is not to do in its current circumstances. And it is by no means accidental that today the late Heidegger has obvious appeal for people who are not simply posing as Greens, but who truly are Greens.

NOTES

1. "Brief über den 'Humanismus,'" *Wegmarken*, 2nd ed. (Frankfurt: Klostermann, 1978), p. 311 ["Letter on Humanism," *Basic Writings*, rev. ed., ed. David Farrell Krell (San Francisco: Harper and Row, 1993), p. 217].

2. Ibid., p. 350 [pp. 255f.]: "disciplines . . . more disciplined . . ."

3. Ibid., p. 349 [p. 255].

4. *Sein und Zeit*, p. 12.

5. Martin Heidegger, *Logik: Die Frage nach der Wahrheit, Gesamtausgabe* Vol. 21 (Frankfurt: Klostermann, 1976), p. 220. See also Gerold Prauss, *Kant über Freiheit als Autonomie* (Frankfurt: Klostermann, 1983), pp. 143ff.

6. Cf. *Sein und Zeit*, p. 193.

7. Ibid., sections 14ff. and pp. 357ff. See also Gerold Prauss, *Knowing and Doing in Heidegger's "Being and Time,"* pp. 4, 9f., 16f., and 20–25 above.

8. Cf. Heidegger, "Vom Wesen des Grundes," *Wegmarken*, 2nd ed., p. 154n. [*The Essence of Reasons*, bilingual ed., trans. Terence Malick (Evanston: Northwestern University, 1969), p. 81n.].
9. Cf., e.g., Heidegger, "Was heißt Denken?" *Vorträge und Aufsätze*, 4th ed. (Pfullingen: Neske, 1978), p. 124 ["What Calls for Thinking?" *Basic Writings*, p. 370]: "It could be that prevailing man has for centuries now acted too much and thought too little." cf. also the deprecation of human action to mere "human making" (*Machenschaft des Menschen*). "Das Ding," *Vorträge und Aufsätze*, 4th ed., p. 174 ["The Thing," *Poetry, Language, Thought*, trans. Albert Hofstadter (New York: Harper and Row, 1971), p. 181].
10. *Sein und Zeit*, p. 358.
11. Ibid., pp. 25f., 33, 61, 138, 158, 170, 357ff.
12. "Wissenschaft und Besinnung," *Vorträge und Aufsätze*, 4th ed., p. 52 ("Science and Reflection," *The Question Concerning Technology and Other Essays*, trans. William Lovitt (New York: Harper Colophon, 1977), p. 167].
13. Cf., e.g., *Sein und Zeit*, p. 357.
14. Ibid., p. 363.
15. Ibid., pp. 149, 359.
16. Ibid., pp. 149, 163f.
17. Ibid., p. 138.
18. Ibid., section 16.
19. Ibid., p. 261 (Macquarrie and Robinson translation altered).
20. Cf. Heidegger, *Logik: Die Frage nach der Wahrheit*, sections 23-27. *Die Grundprobleme der Phänomenologie, Gesamtausgabe*, Vol. 24 (Frankfurt: Klostermann, 1975) [*The Basic Problems of Phenomenology*, rev. ed., trans. Albert Hofstadter (Bloomington: Indiana University, 1988)].
21. Cf. *The Basic Problems of Phenomenology*, sections 9, 15, 17–18. Accordingly he seems increasingly to exclude Kant from the general criticism that modernity has failed to recognize intentionality as the essence of subjectivity; cf. *Logik: Die Frage nach der Wahrheit*, p. 290.
22. Notwithstanding occasional statements to the contrary (cf., e.g., *Die Grundprobleme der Phänomenologie*, pp. 83ff. [*The Basic Problems of Phenomenology*, pp. 59ff.]), which are made under a Kantian influence that is never permanent.
23. Cf. *Die Grundprobleme der Phänomenologie*, pp. 90f. with pp. 101ff., and pp. 237ff., 294ff. [*The Basic Problems of Phenomenology*, pp. 64f. with 71ff., and pp. 166ff., 206ff].
24. Cf. Kant, *Kritik der reinen Vernunft, Kants gesammelte Schriften*, Akademie Ausgabe (Berlin: De Gruyter, 1902-) Vol. III, B110.
25. Cf., e.g., "Das Ding," p. 174 ["The Thing," p. 181].
26. Cf., e.g., "Brief über den 'Humanismus,'" p. 339 ["Letter on Humanism," p. 246]; "Das Ding," pp. 174, 178 ["The Thing," pp. 181, 185].
27. Cf. "Brief über den 'Humanismus,'" p. 354 ["Letter on Humanism," p. 259].
28. Ibid., p. 311 [p. 217].
29. Ibid., p. 349 [p. 254].
30. "Überwindung der Metaphysik," *Vorträge und Aufsätze*, 4th ed., p. 90.
31. Cf., e.g., "Überwindung der Metaphysik," p. 68: "That human beings, as *animal rationale*, i.e. as the living beings that labor, must wander through the desert of the devastation of the earth. . . ."
32. "Brief über den 'Humanismus,'" p. 349 ["Letter on Humanism," p. 255 (translation altered slightly)].
33. Ibid., p. 311 with 349ff., and p. 353 [p. 217 with 254ff., and p. 258].
34. Ibid., pp. 348f. [p. 254].

Index

actual/actuality: and concern, 19, 20; and Dasein, 47; and doing, xiii, 38–41, 42, 44; and intention, 69; and knowing, xiii, xiv, 40–41, 42, 44, 65; *vs.* possible, 38

actualization, 19, 39, 40, 42, 43, 69

aesthetics, 52, 53, 57, 58

aletheia (ἀ-λήζεια), 52

antiquity, 52, 70

Aristotle, viii, x, 8, 9, 48, 51, 53n. 1, 65, 66

Aschenberg, Reinhold, xvi, xvii–xviii

assertion, 15, 16, 17, 18

as-structure, 15

autonomy, xiv, 71, 72

awaiting, 20, 21

backwardness: *See* utopia/utopian

Basic Problems of Phenomenology, The (Heidegger), 73nn. 20, 22, 23

beauty/ugliness, 53

Being and Time (Heidegger), passim

Being-in-itself, 36

beyond, going or being, 39–40, 41, 42, 53

bifurcation, 57, 59, 61

Bollnow, Otto Friedrich, 5n. 1

Brentano, Franz, viii, 68

Bröcker, Walter, x, xi, 9

care, 64. *See also* concern

change-over, from circumspective to non-circumspective knowing, xi, 4, 7, 13, 16, 20, 25, 66

circumspection: change over from, 4, 7, 13, 16, 20, 25, 66; and concern, x, xi, 7, 28, 29; disturbed, 67; and disturbed concern, 27, 28; falsity in, 17; going wrong in, 28, 29, 66–67; and knowing, xi–xii, 4, 14, 28–29, 33, 35, 47–48, 51, 65, 66; making present of, 21; and natural science, 9–10; negative evaluation of, 50; observation as, 3; and perception, xi, 15, 17, 30; as practical knowing, 14; of practice, 13; practicist theory of, 47; as pre-predicative, 66; and present-at-hand, xii, xv, xvi–xvii, 28–29; present of, 21; and ready-to-hand, xi, 15, 16, 20–21; and success/failure, xii, 29; and theory, 32, 42, 48; as true or false, 67; as undisturbed, 33

concern: and circumspection, x, xi, 26; Dasein as, 65; deficient modes of, xii, 2, 18, 26; "disturbed," 25–34, 37, 67; and doing, x, 1–4, 19, 29; emergence of, 20–21; as intention, 19, 23n. 3; and knowing, x, 1–4, 7, 19; and making present, 21; practical, 64; and present-at-hand, 7; as success or failure, xii, 27, 67; theory of, 13, 18

conscience, 62n. 2

critical rationalism, xiii, 58, 62n. 4

critical theory, xiii, 58, 59, 62n. 4

manipulation, 4

Marx, Karl, xii, 32

material, 43

materialism, xiii, 58, 61

means: action as, 34, 39; and beings "in themselves," 37; Dasein as, 36; knowing as, xii, xvi, 34, 35–36; and means-ends relation, 35, 37, 71

metaphor, xiii, xvi, 30, 34n. 1, 41, 49

mistake, 29

modernity, 52, 68, 70

morality, x, xiii, xiv, 62n. 2, 63. See also ethics

moral law, xiv, 61

moral philosophy, 58

National Socialism, vii

naturalness (of Dasein or the subject), 57

natural science: and knowing, 4, 16, 21, 48, 51, 65; origin of, 21; and subjectivity, 52, 68; and technology, xi, 7, 9, 10, 13, 14, 51, 60, 65–66, 68; and theoria, xi, 66

neediness (of Dasein), 40

Neo-Kantians, 68, 69. See also German Idealism

noema/noesis, xii, xiii, xiv, xv, xvii, 31, 43–45, 52, 59

object, 64

objectification, 21, 65, 66, 69

objectivity, ix, x, 43, 58, 59, 62n. 4

observing that strives after, 54n. 6

obsession with success, ix, xviii, 57, 58, 60, 61, 62n. 2. See also success/ failure

"On the Essence of Truth" (Heidegger), 50

perception/perceiving: and aesthetics, 53; and circumspection, xi, 15, 17, 30; and error, 17, 29, 67; and knowing, 2, 48, 52, 65; and present-at-hand, 29; and ready-to-hand, 29; receptivity of, xiii, 48, 49, 51, 54n. 4; of something as something,

15, 16; and subjectivity of Dasein, 49; and success, 47; as true or false, 17, 30; unarticulated, 17

Pöggeler, Otto, 22

poiema/poiesis, xiii, xiv, 43–45, 59

possibility, 19–20, 38

practical dealing, 17, 64

practical knowing, 14

Practical Philosophy, viii, xiv, xviii, 63, 64, 70

practical reason, viii

practice: disappearance of, 4; and natural science, 7–8; primacy of theory over, x, 17, 25, 42; primacy over theory, 1, 2, 13, 42, 43, 58, 65; and subjectivity, xxiii

practicism: and critical theory, 58; departure from, 48, 51, 52, 57; of knowing and truth, xiii, 47; and materialism, 58; in Prauss, xv–xvi; and subjectivity, 60, 61

practicity, viii, ix, x, xiv, xv, 68, 69–70

Prauss, Gerold: Erscheinung bei Kant. Ein Problem der "Kritik der reinen Vernunft," xxn. 20; Heidegger and Practical Philosophy, xiv; Kant über Freiheit als Autonomie, xixn. 11, 72n. 5; Kant und das problem der Dinge an Sich, xxn. 20; Die Welt und wir, xixn. 11, xxn. 20

predication/predicative, 16, 29, 66

pre-predicative, xi, 15–16, 29, 66

present-at-hand: and change-over, 20–21, 23n. 3; and circumspection, xii, xv, xvi–xvii, 25, 35, 47–48; and consideration of present-at-hand, 18; and knowing, xi, xii, 4, 7, 8, 9, 10, 14, 15, 16, 20–21, 54n. 7; objectification of, 65, 66; and perception, 29; positive evaluation of, 50–51; primacy of ready-to-hand over, x, 2, 3, 17, 64; and theory, 48; thing as, 64. See also ready-to-hand

producing, 2, 8, 18, 19, 39, 69